Ivan Kushnir

Economy of the Solomon Islands

Series "Economy in countries"

first published: 2019
last updated: 2021-01-26

Ivan Kushnir. Economy of the Solomon Islands. Series "Economy in countries". - 2019. - 71 pages.

This book about the economy of the Solomon Islands from the 1970s to the 2010s. Source data from UN Data.

Size. In the 2010s, the gross domestic product of the Solomon Islands was equal to $1.1 billion per year; the value of agriculture was $300.5 million; the value of industry was $123.0 million. Since the share in the world is less than .01%, the country is classified as a micro economy.

Productivity. In the 2010s, the GDP per capita was $1 800.1, the value of agriculture per capita was $503.7, the value of industry per capita was $206.1. Since the productivity is less the average below average, the economy is classified as least developed.

Growth. In the 2010s, the growth of gross domestic product was 4.3%; the growth of agriculture was 3.9%; the growth of industry was 2.7%.

Structure. In the 2010s, the economy of the Solomon Islands included: services (31.1%), agriculture (26.8%), trade (21.2%), industry (11.0%), transportation (5.6%), and construction (4.4%).

Exports and imports. In the 2010s, the imports were 19.9% higher than the exports, the net imports were equal to 10.6% of the GDP. The technological structure of exports are not better than the structure of imports.

Consumption and reproduction. The attitude of reproduction to the consumption is not better than the global average, so the share of GDP in the world will not increase.

Series "Economy in countries": parallel.page.link/en

ISBN: 9781795310383

Contents

Part I. Size

	The 2010s
GDP	$1.1 billion
The share in the world	0.0014%
Share in Oceania	0.065%
Share in Melanesia	2.9%

Chapter I. Gross domestic product

The Solomon Islands GDP enlarged from $67.5 million per year in the 1970s to $1.1 billion per year in the 2010s, that is by $1.0 billion or 15.9 times. The change occurred at $772.9 million due to a 3.6-fold increase in prices, as also at $89.6 million due to a 1.4-fold increase in productivity, as well as at $143.8 million due to the expansion in population. The average annual growth in GDP is 4.1%. The minimum value of gross domestic product was in 1970 at $32.0 million. The maximum value of gross domestic product was in 2018 at $1.3 billion.

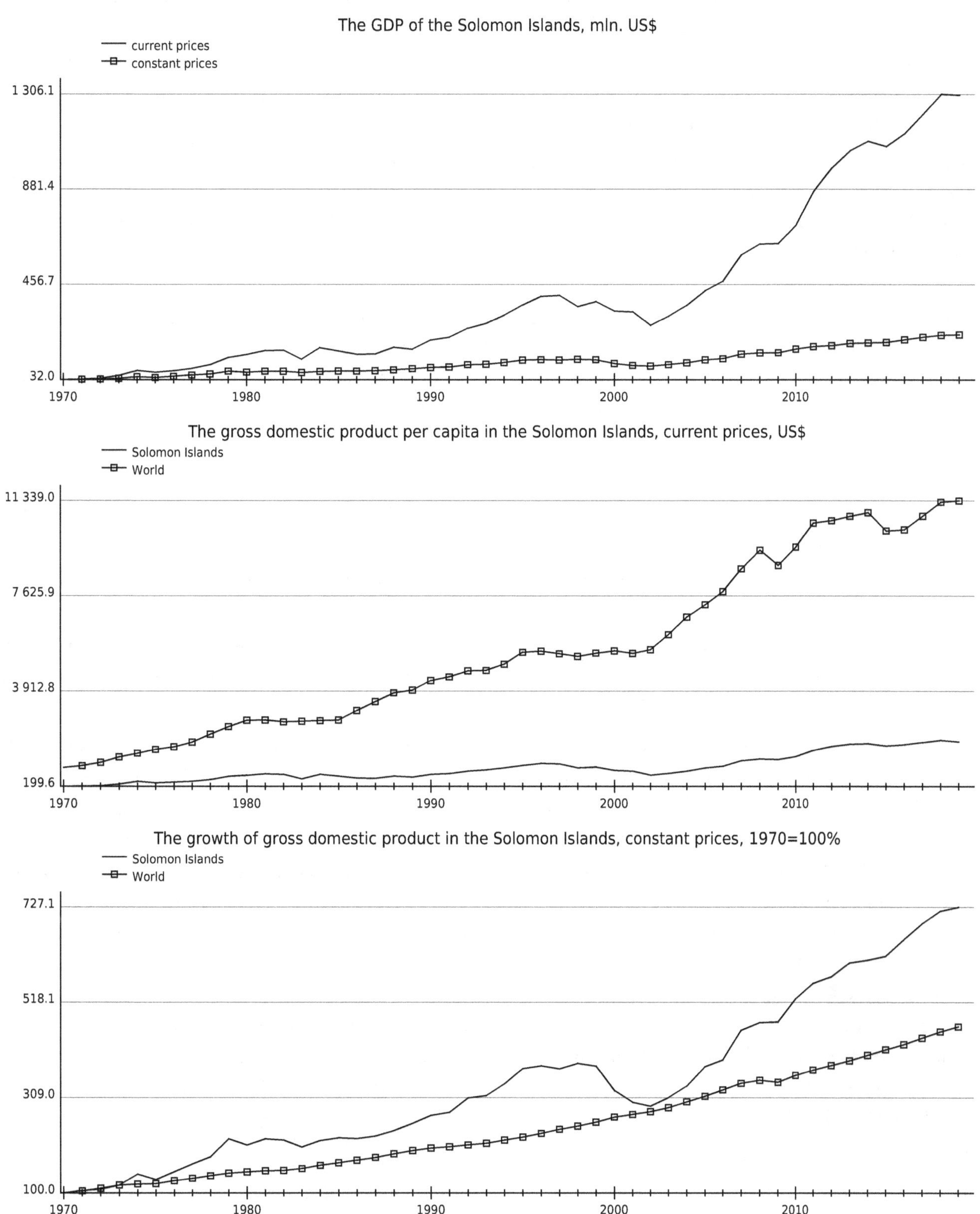

The 1970s

The GDP of the Solomon Islands was $67.5 million per year in the 1970s, ranked 165th in the world. The share in the world was 0.0010%, and 0.059% in Oceania.

The GDP of the Solomon Islands included: household expenditure (57.4%), government consumption expenditure (23.0%), and capital formation (21.9%).

The Solomon Islands GDP per capita was $354.2 in the 1970s, ranked 147th in the world, and was on a par with Liberia ($355.7), Egypt ($347.3). The Solomon Islands GDP per capita was less than gross domestic product per capita in the world ($1 620.8) in 4.6 times, and was less than gross domestic product per capita in Oceania ($5 398.2) in 15.2 times.

The growth of GDP in the Solomon Islands was 9.1% in the 1970s, ranked 17th in the world, and was on a par with Aruba (9.1%). The growth of gross domestic product in the Solomon Islands (9.1%) was greater than growth of gross domestic product in the world (4.1%), was greater than growth of GDP in Oceania (2.8%).

Comparison with neighbors. The Solomon Islands gross domestic product was greater than in Nauru ($28.8 million); but less than in Papua New Guinea ($2.3 billion), in New Caledonia ($685.9 million), and in Vanuatu ($73.5 million). The GDP per capita in the Solomon Islands was less than in New Caledonia ($5.4 thousand), in Nauru ($4.1 thousand), in Papua New Guinea ($747.7), and in Vanuatu ($745.9). The growth of GDP in the Solomon Islands was greater than in Vanuatu (7.7%), in Papua New Guinea (1.7%), in New Caledonia (1.7%), and in Nauru (0.32%).

Comparison with leaders. The GDP of the Solomon Islands was less than in the USA ($1.7 trillion), in the USSR ($649.4 billion), in Japan ($558.0 billion), in Germany ($484.2 billion), and in France ($333.2 billion). The GDP per capita in the Solomon Islands was less than in the USA ($7.8 thousand), in France ($6.2 thousand), in Germany ($6.1 thousand), in Japan ($5.0 thousand), and in the USSR ($2.6 thousand). The growth of GDP in the Solomon Islands was greater than in the USSR (4.8%), in Japan (4.6%), in France (3.9%), in the United States (3.5%), and in Germany (3.1%).

The 1980s

The GDP of the Solomon Islands was $156.0 million per year in the 1980s, ranked 165th in the world. The share in the world was 0.0010%, and 0.061% in Oceania.

The gross domestic product of the Solomon Islands included: household expenditure (62.6%), government consumption expenditure (29.2%), and capital formation (25.7%).

The Solomon Islands GDP per capita was $585.0 in the 1980s, ranked 142nd in the world, and was on a par with Kiribati ($571.4). The GDP per capita in the Solomon Islands was less than GDP per capita in the world ($3 123.4) in 5.3 times, and was less than GDP per capita in Oceania ($10 390.7) in 17.8 times.

The growth of gross domestic product in the Solomon Islands was 1.5% in the 1980s, ranked 141st in the world. The growth of GDP in the Solomon Islands (1.5%) was less than growth of gross domestic product in the world (3.0%), was less than growth of gross domestic product in Oceania (3.1%).

Comparison with neighbors. The Solomon Islands GDP was greater than in Vanuatu ($131.1 million) and in Nauru ($40.2 million); but less than in Papua New Guinea ($4.4 billion) and in New Caledonia ($1.2 billion). The Solomon Islands GDP per capita was less than in New Caledonia ($8.0 thousand), in Nauru ($4.8 thousand), in Papua New Guinea ($1 092.2), and in Vanuatu ($1 017.9). The growth of GDP in the Solomon Islands was greater than in Papua New Guinea (1.4%) and in Nauru (-2.8%); but less than in New Caledonia (4.5%) and in Vanuatu (4.1%).

Comparison with leaders. The Solomon Islands GDP was less than in the USA ($4.2 trillion), in Japan ($1.8 trillion), in Germany ($990.0 billion), in the USSR ($887.0 billion), and in France ($729.5 billion). The Solomon Islands gross domestic product per capita was less than in the USA ($17.4 thousand), in Japan ($15.0 thousand), in France ($12.9 thousand), in Germany ($12.7 thousand), and in the USSR ($3.2 thousand). The growth of GDP in the Solomon Islands was less than in the USSR (4.3%), in Japan (4.3%), in the USA (3.1%), in France (2.3%), and in Germany (1.9%).

The 1990s

The gross domestic product of the Solomon Islands was $320.6 million per year in the 1990s, ranked 189th in the world. The share in the world was 0.0011%, and 0.072% in Oceania.

The gross domestic product of the Solomon Islands included: household expenditure (49.8%), government consumption expenditure (32.2%), and capital formation (19.8%).

The GDP per capita in the Solomon Islands was $902.5 in the 1990s, ranked 142nd in the world, and was on a par with Nicaragua ($899.0), Central Asia ($891.5). The Solomon Islands gross domestic product per capita was less than GDP per capita in the world ($5 020.1) in 5.6 times, and was less than GDP per capita in Oceania ($15 413.2) in 17.1 times.

The growth of gross domestic product in the Solomon Islands was 4.1% in the 1990s, ranked 68th in the world, and was on a par with Guatemala (4.1%). The growth of gross domestic product in the Solomon Islands (4.1%) was greater than growth of GDP in the world (2.8%), was greater than growth of GDP in Oceania (3.3%).

Comparison with neighbors. The Solomon Islands gross domestic product was greater than in Vanuatu ($241.5 million) and in Nauru ($35.9 million); but less than in Papua New Guinea ($6.6 billion) and in New Caledonia ($3.2 billion). The gross domestic product per capita in the Solomon Islands was less than in New Caledonia ($16.7 thousand), in Nauru ($3.5 thousand), in Vanuatu ($1 463.0), and in Papua New Guinea ($1 291.0). The growth of GDP in the Solomon Islands was greater than in Vanuatu (3.5%), in New Caledonia (2.1%), and in Nauru (-10.7%); but less than in Papua New Guinea (4.5%).

Comparison with leaders. The GDP of the Solomon Islands was less than in the USA ($7.6 trillion), in Japan ($4.3 trillion), in Germany ($2.2 trillion), in France ($1.4 trillion), and in the United Kingdom ($1.3 trillion). The Solomon Islands gross domestic product per capita was less than in Japan ($34.3 thousand), in the United States ($28.7 thousand), in Germany ($27.0 thousand), in France ($24.1 thousand), and in the UK ($22.9 thousand). The growth of GDP in the Solomon Islands was greater than in the USA (3.2%), in the UK (2.3%), in Germany (2.2%), in France (2.0%), and in Japan (1.5%).

The 2000s

The GDP of the Solomon Islands was $438.9 million per year in the 2000s, ranked 196th in the world, and was on a par with Samoa ($434.4 million). The share in the world was 0.0009%, and 0.053% in Oceania.

The GDP of the Solomon Islands included: household expenditure (60.5%), government expenditure (34.5%), and capital formation (16.5%).

The Solomon Islands gross domestic product per capita was $945.9 in the 2000s, ranked 164th in the world, and was on a par with Sudan ($944.3), Djibouti ($952.5), Yemen ($955.0). The gross domestic product per capita in the Solomon Islands was less than gross domestic product per capita in the world ($7 176.3) in 7.6 times, and was less than GDP per capita in Oceania ($24 984.1) in 26.4 times.

The growth of gross domestic product in the Solomon Islands was 2.3% in the 2000s, ranked 156th in the world, and was on a par with Grenada (2.3%), Argentina (2.3%). The growth of GDP in the Solomon Islands (2.3%) was less than growth of GDP in the world (3.0%), was less than growth of gross domestic product in Oceania (3.0%).

Comparison with neighbors. The Solomon Islands gross domestic product was greater than in Vanuatu ($404.2 million) and in Nauru ($28.2 million); but less than in Papua New Guinea ($7.5 billion) and in New Caledonia ($6.1 billion). The Solomon Islands gross domestic product per capita was less than in New Caledonia ($26.0 thousand), in Nauru ($2.8 thousand), in Vanuatu ($1 953.5), and in Papua New Guinea ($1 161.8). The growth of gross domestic product in the Solomon Islands was greater than in Nauru (-1.6%); but less than in Vanuatu (3.6%), in New Caledonia (3.2%), and in Papua New Guinea (2.5%).

Comparison with leaders. The Solomon Islands GDP was less than in the USA ($12.6 trillion), in Japan ($4.7 trillion), in Germany ($2.8 trillion), in China ($2.6 trillion), and in the UK ($2.3 trillion). The Solomon Islands gross domestic product per capita was less than in the USA ($42.8 thousand), in the United Kingdom ($38.4 thousand), in Japan ($36.4 thousand), in Germany ($34.0 thousand), and in China ($1 954.1). The growth of GDP in the Solomon Islands was greater than in the United States (1.9%), in the United Kingdom (1.7%), in Germany (0.73%), and in Japan (0.50%); but less than in China (10.3%).

The 2010s

The GDP of the Solomon Islands was $1.1 billion per year in the 2010s, ranked 191st in the world, and was on a par with Micronesia ($1.1 billion), the Comoros ($1.1 billion). The share in the world was 0.0014%, and 0.065% in Oceania.

The GDP of the Solomon Islands consisted of: household expenditure (59.3%), government consumption expenditure (31.4%), and capital formation (18.6%).

The GDP per capita in the Solomon Islands was $1 800.1 in the 2010s, ranked 163rd in the world, and was on a par with Southern Asia ($1 801.7), Sudan ($1 833.1). The gross domestic product per capita in the Solomon Islands was less than gross domestic product per capita in the world ($10 603.1) in 5.9 times, and was less than gross domestic product per capita in Oceania ($42 253.4) in 23.5 times.

The growth of gross domestic product in the Solomon Islands was 4.3% in the 2010s, ranked 64th in the world, and was on a par with Paraguay (4.4%), Malawi (4.4%). The growth of gross domestic product in the Solomon Islands (4.3%) was greater than growth of GDP in the world (3.1%), was greater than growth of GDP in Oceania (2.5%).

Comparison with neighbors. The Solomon Islands gross domestic product was 31.6% higher than in Vanuatu ($815.7 million) and 9.4 times higher than in Nauru ($114.1 million); but 19.8 times lower than in Papua New Guinea ($21.2 billion) and 9.1 times lower than in New Caledonia ($9.7 billion). The Solomon Islands GDP per capita was 20.1 times lower than in New Caledonia ($36.2 thousand), 6.1 times lower than in Nauru ($11.0 thousand), 40.9% lower than in Vanuatu ($3.0 thousand), and 31.9% lower than in Papua New Guinea ($2.6 thousand). The growth of gross domestic product in the Solomon Islands was greater than in New Caledonia (2.4%) and in Vanuatu (2.3%); but less than in Nauru (10.6%) and in Papua New Guinea (5.4%).

Comparison with leaders. The Solomon Islands GDP was 16 727.6 times lower than in the USA ($18.0 trillion), 9 784.3 times lower than in China ($10.5 trillion), 4 869.1 times lower than in Japan ($5.2 trillion), 3 410.0 times lower than in Germany ($3.7 trillion), and 2 576.6 times lower than in the United Kingdom ($2.8 trillion). The GDP per capita in the Solomon Islands was 31.2 times lower than in the USA ($56.2 thousand), 24.9 times lower than in Germany ($44.7 thousand), 23.4 times lower than in the United Kingdom ($42.2 thousand), 22.7 times lower than in Japan ($40.9 thousand), and 4.2 times lower than in China ($7.5 thousand). The growth of GDP in the Solomon Islands was greater than in the United States (2.3%), in Germany (1.9%), in the United Kingdom (1.8%), and in Japan (1.3%); but less than in China (7.7%).

Chapter II. Value added

The value added of the Solomon Islands increased from $60.5 million per year in the 1970s to $1.1 billion per year in the 2010s, that is by $1.1 billion or 18.6 times. The change occurred at $830.5 million due to a 3.8-fold increase in prices, as also at $102.3 million due to a 1.5-fold increase in productivity, as well as at $128.9 million due to the rise in population. The average annual growth in value added is 4.4%. The minimum value of value added was in 1970 at $28.7 million. The maximum value of value added was in 2019 at $1.4 billion.

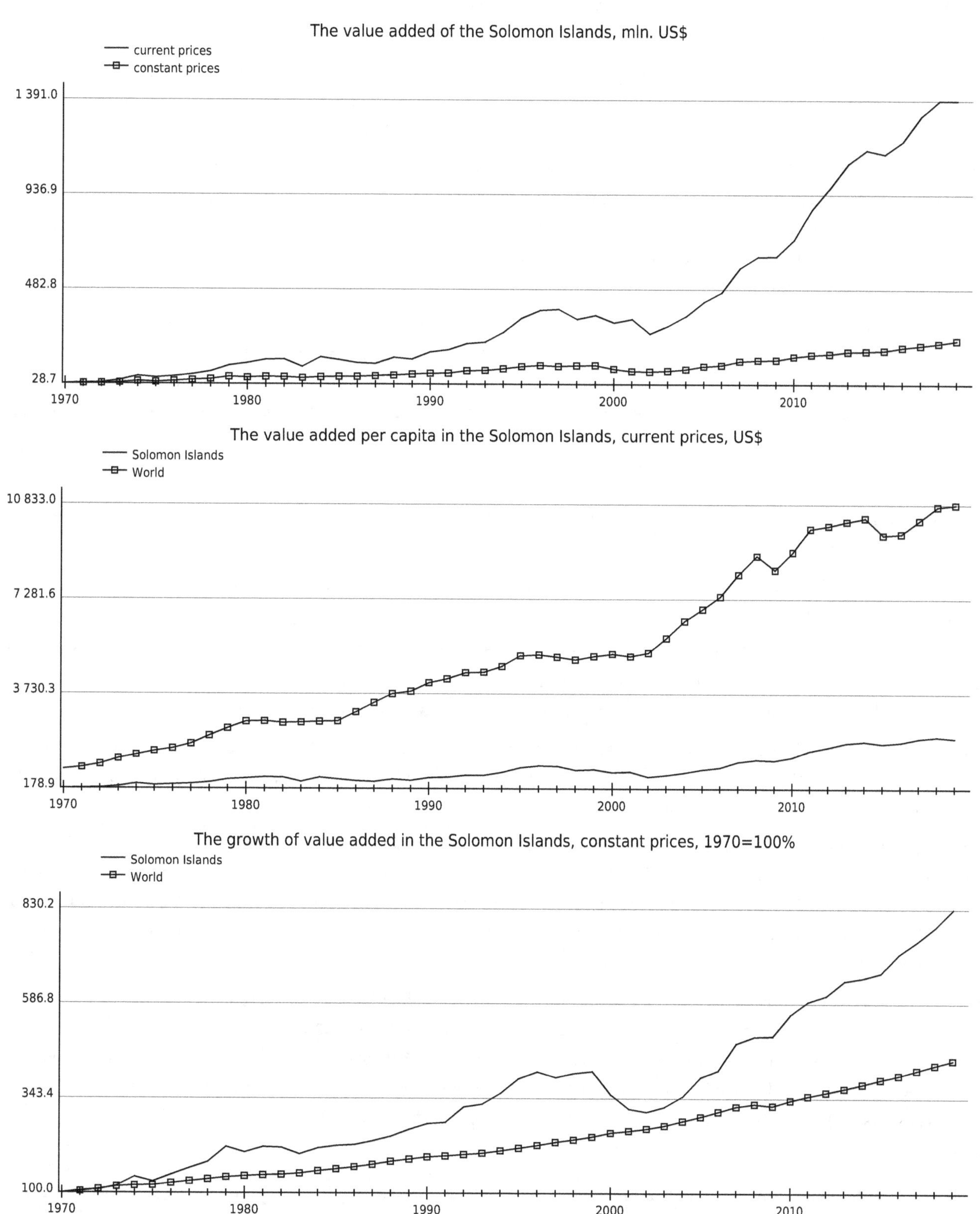

The 1970s

The value added of the Solomon Islands was $60.5 million per year in the 1970s, ranked 165th in the world. The share in the world was 0.0010%, and 0.056% in Oceania.

The total value added of the Solomon Islands included: agriculture (51.6%), services (24.5%), trade (10.2%), transportation (5.3%), industry (4.2%), and construction (4.2%).

The Solomon Islands value added per capita was $317.4 in the 1970s, ranked 149th in the world, and was on a par with Egypt ($318.1), Liberia ($323.2). The value added per capita in the Solomon Islands was less than value added per capita in the world ($1 564.4) in 4.9 times, and was less than value added per capita in Oceania ($5 074.3) in 16.0 times.

The growth of value added in the Solomon Islands was 9.1% in the 1970s, ranked 14th in the world, and was on a par with Republic of Korea (9.0%), Aruba (9.1%), Brazil (9.2%). The growth of value added in the Solomon Islands (9.1%) was greater than growth of value added in the world (3.9%), was greater than growth of value added in Oceania (3.2%).

Comparison with neighbors. The Solomon Islands value added was greater than in Nauru ($31.0 million); but less than in Papua New Guinea ($2.7 billion), in New Caledonia ($686.4 million), and in Vanuatu ($69.6 million). The Solomon Islands value added per capita was less than in New Caledonia ($5.4 thousand), in Nauru ($4.4 thousand), in Papua New Guinea ($851.5), and in Vanuatu ($706.2). The growth of value added in the Solomon Islands was greater than in Vanuatu (7.7%), in Papua New Guinea (2.9%), in New Caledonia (1.7%), and in Nauru (0.37%).

Comparison with leaders. The Solomon Islands value added was less than in the United States ($1.7 trillion), in the USSR ($649.4 billion), in Japan ($545.3 billion), in Germany ($444.9 billion), and in France ($297.3 billion). The value added per capita in the Solomon Islands was less than in the USA ($7.8 thousand), in Germany ($5.7 thousand), in France ($5.5 thousand), in Japan ($4.9 thousand), and in the USSR ($2.6 thousand). The growth of value added in the Solomon Islands was greater than in Japan (4.9%), in the USSR (4.8%), in France (3.7%), in Germany (3.1%), and in the USA (2.9%).

The 1980s

The Solomon Islands value added was $138.7 million per year in the 1980s, ranked 165th in the world. The share in the world was 0.0009%, and 0.057% in Oceania.

The total value added of the Solomon Islands consisted of: agriculture (49.7%), services (25.8%), trade (10.6%), transportation (5.4%), construction (4.4%), and industry (4.1%).

The value added per capita in the Solomon Islands was $520.1 in the 1980s, ranked 145th in the world, and was on a par with Kiribati ($515.9), Kenya ($511.7), Mongolia ($531.4). The value added per capita in the Solomon Islands was less than value added per capita in the world ($3 029.9) in 5.8 times, and was less than value added per capita in Oceania ($9 797.7) in 18.8 times.

The growth of value added in the Solomon Islands was 1.9% in the 1980s, ranked 132nd in the world, and was on a par with Melanesia (1.9%), Czechoslovakia (1.9%), New Zealand (1.9%). The growth of value added in the Solomon Islands (1.9%) was less than growth of value added in the world (2.9%), was less than growth of value added in Oceania (3.4%).

Comparison with neighbors. The Solomon Islands value added was greater than in Vanuatu ($131.2 million) and in Nauru ($43.2 million); but less than in Papua New Guinea ($4.9 billion) and in New Caledonia ($1.2 billion). The value added per capita in the Solomon Islands was less than in New Caledonia ($8.0 thousand), in Nauru ($5.1 thousand), in Papua New Guinea ($1 221.0), and in Vanuatu ($1 018.4). The growth of value added in the Solomon Islands was greater than in Papua New Guinea (0.71%) and in Nauru (-2.8%); but less than in New Caledonia (4.5%) and in Vanuatu (3.7%).

Comparison with leaders. The value added of the Solomon Islands was less than in the United States ($4.2 trillion), in Japan ($1.8 trillion), in Germany ($907.0 billion), in the USSR ($887.0 billion), and in France ($650.9 billion). The value added per capita in the Solomon Islands was less than in the USA ($17.4 thousand), in Japan ($14.8 thousand), in Germany ($11.6 thousand), in France ($11.5 thousand), and in the USSR ($3.2 thousand). The growth of value added in the Solomon Islands was less than in the USSR (4.3%), in Japan (4.2%), in the United States (2.8%), in France (2.2%), and in Germany (2.0%).

The 1990s

The value added of the Solomon Islands was $291.8 million per year in the 1990s, ranked 189th in the world, and was on a par with

Bhutan ($286.3 million). The share in the world was 0.0011%, and 0.071% in Oceania.

The total value added of the Solomon Islands included: agriculture (41.8%), services (29.2%), industry (9.6%), trade (9.5%), transportation (6.7%), and construction (3.2%).

The value added per capita in the Solomon Islands was $821.4 in the 1990s, ranked 145th in the world, and was on a par with Ghana ($822.3), Nicaragua ($808.2), Bolivia ($804.4). The Solomon Islands value added per capita was less than value added per capita in the world ($4 799.9) in 5.8 times, and was less than value added per capita in Oceania ($14 241.8) in 17.3 times.

The growth of value added in the Solomon Islands was 4.6% in the 1990s, ranked 50th in the world, and was on a par with Mozambique (4.6%), Asia (4.6%), El Salvador (4.6%). The growth of value added in the Solomon Islands (4.6%) was greater than growth of value added in the world (2.7%), was greater than growth of value added in Oceania (3.3%).

Comparison with neighbors. The value added of the Solomon Islands was greater than in Vanuatu ($227.0 million) and in Nauru ($38.7 million); but less than in Papua New Guinea ($6.9 billion) and in New Caledonia ($3.1 billion). The Solomon Islands value added per capita was less than in New Caledonia ($16.3 thousand), in Nauru ($3.8 thousand), in Vanuatu ($1 375.1), and in Papua New Guinea ($1 340.3). The growth of value added in the Solomon Islands was greater than in Papua New Guinea (4.5%), in Vanuatu (2.7%), in New Caledonia (1.3%), and in Nauru (-10.8%).

Comparison with leaders. The Solomon Islands value added was less than in the United States ($7.6 trillion), in Japan ($4.3 trillion), in Germany ($2.0 trillion), in France ($1.3 trillion), and in the United Kingdom ($1.2 trillion). The value added per capita in the Solomon Islands was less than in Japan ($34.2 thousand), in the United States ($28.6 thousand), in Germany ($24.5 thousand), in France ($21.6 thousand), and in the UK ($21.4 thousand). The growth of value added in the Solomon Islands was greater than in the USA (2.8%), in the UK (2.4%), in Germany (2.1%), in France (1.8%), and in Japan (1.8%).

The 2000s

The Solomon Islands value added was $435.2 million per year in the 2000s, ranked 196th in the world, and was on a par with Samoa ($434.1 million). The share in the world was 0.0010%, and 0.057% in Oceania.

The total value added of the Solomon Islands included: services (35.1%), agriculture (30.7%), trade (14.6%), transportation (8.6%), industry (8.4%), and construction (2.5%).

The Solomon Islands value added per capita was $938.0 in the 2000s, ranked 161st in the world, and was on a par with Yemen ($943.0), Cameroon ($929.5), Sudan ($924.8). The value added per capita in the Solomon Islands was less than value added per capita in the world ($6 818.0) in 7.3 times, and was less than value added per capita in Oceania ($23 074.9) in 24.6 times.

The growth of value added in the Solomon Islands was 2% in the 2000s, ranked 159th in the world, and was on a par with Liechtenstein (2.0%), Monaco (2.0%). The growth of value added in the Solomon Islands (2.0%) was less than growth of value added in the world (2.9%), was less than growth of value added in Oceania (3.0%).

Comparison with neighbors. The Solomon Islands value added was greater than in Vanuatu ($371.7 million) and in Nauru ($28.8 million); but less than in Papua New Guinea ($7.2 billion) and in New Caledonia ($5.6 billion). The Solomon Islands value added per capita was less than in New Caledonia ($24.0 thousand), in Nauru ($2.9 thousand), in Vanuatu ($1 796.2), and in Papua New Guinea ($1 115.8). The growth of value added in the Solomon Islands was greater than in Papua New Guinea (1.7%) and in Nauru (-2.0%); but less than in Vanuatu (3.4%) and in New Caledonia (3.2%).

Comparison with leaders. The value added of the Solomon Islands was less than in the United States ($12.6 trillion), in Japan ($4.7 trillion), in China ($2.6 trillion), in Germany ($2.5 trillion), and in the UK ($2.1 trillion). The Solomon Islands value added per capita was less than in the United States ($42.8 thousand), in Japan ($36.4 thousand), in the UK ($34.6 thousand), in Germany ($30.7 thousand), and in China ($1 954.1). The growth of value added in the Solomon Islands was greater than in the United States (1.7%), in the UK (1.7%), in Germany (0.65%), and in Japan (0.27%); but less than in China (10.2%).

The 2010s

The Solomon Islands value added was $1.1 billion per year in the 2010s, ranked 189th in the world, and was on a par with the Seychelles ($1.1 billion), Guinea-Bissau ($1.1 billion). The share in the world was 0.0015%, and 0.073% in Oceania.

The total value added of the Solomon Islands included: services (31.1%), agriculture (26.8%), trade (21.2%), industry (11.0%), transportation (5.6%), and construction (4.4%).

The Solomon Islands value added per capita was $1 881.1 in the 2010s, ranked 158th in the world, and was on a par with Africa ($1 886.4), Ghana ($1 897.8), Uzbekistan ($1 899.4). The value added per capita in the Solomon Islands was less than value added per capita in the world ($10 094.6) in 5.4 times, and was less than value added per capita in Oceania ($39 391.3) in 20.9 times.

The growth of value added in the Solomon Islands was 5.1% in the 2010s, ranked 41st in the world. The growth of value added in the Solomon Islands (5.1%) was greater than growth of value added in the world (3.1%), was greater than growth of value added in Oceania (2.5%).

Comparison with neighbors. The Solomon Islands value added was 47.4% higher than in Vanuatu ($761.1 million) and 9.8 times higher than in Nauru ($114.7 million); but 18.2 times lower than in Papua New Guinea ($20.4 billion) and 8.0 times lower than in New Caledonia ($9.0 billion). The value added per capita in the Solomon Islands was 17.7 times lower than in New Caledonia ($33.4 thousand), 5.9 times lower than in Nauru ($11.1 thousand), 33.9% lower than in Vanuatu ($2.8 thousand), and 25.8% lower than in Papua New Guinea ($2.5 thousand). The growth of value added in the Solomon Islands was greater than in New Caledonia (2.9%) and in Vanuatu (2.6%); but less than in Nauru (9.7%) and in Papua New Guinea (5.6%).

Comparison with leaders. The value added of the Solomon Islands was 16 007.3 times lower than in the United States ($18.0 trillion), 9 362.9 times lower than in China ($10.5 trillion), 4 635.6 times lower than in Japan ($5.2 trillion), 2 943.3 times lower than in Germany ($3.3 trillion), and 2 201.6 times lower than in the United Kingdom ($2.5 trillion). The Solomon Islands value added per capita was 29.9 times lower than in the USA ($56.2 thousand), 21.6 times lower than in Japan ($40.7 thousand), 21.4 times lower than in Germany ($40.3 thousand), 20.0 times lower than in the UK ($37.7 thousand), and 4.0 times lower than in China ($7.5 thousand). The growth of value added in the Solomon Islands was greater than in the United States (2.2%), in Germany (1.9%), in the United Kingdom (1.8%), and in Japan (1.3%); but less than in China (7.7%).

Chapter III. Gross national income

The GNI of the Solomon Islands increased from $66.2 million per year in the 1970s to $976.7 million per year in the 2010s, that is by $910.5 million or 14.7 times. The change occurred at $704.7 million due to a 3.6-fold increase in prices, as also at $64.6 million due to a 1.3-fold increase in productivity, as well as at $141.2 million due to the growth in population. The average annual growth in GNI is 4.1%. The minimum value of gross national income was in 1970 at $31.4 million. The maximum value of GNI was in 2018 at $1.2 billion.

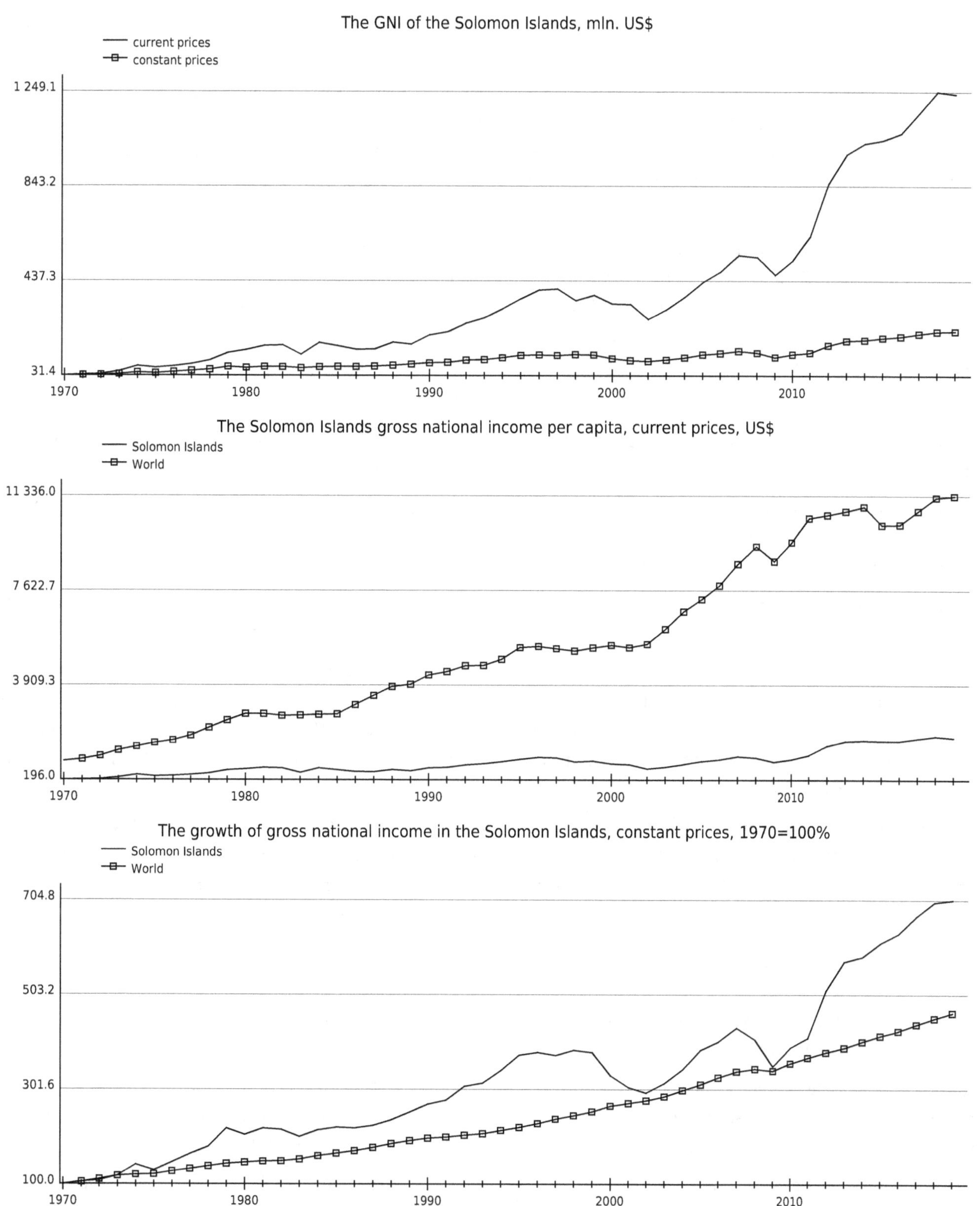

The 1970s

The Solomon Islands gross national income was $66.2 million per year in the 1970s, ranked 165th in the world, and was on a par with Bhutan ($67.9 million). The share in the world was 0.0010%, and 0.058% in Oceania.

The Solomon Islands GNI per capita was $347.7 in the 1970s, ranked 148th in the world, and was on a par with Botswana ($343.3), Egypt ($353.8). The GNI per capita in the Solomon Islands was less than gross national income per capita in the world ($1 624.3) in 4.7 times, and was less than GNI per capita in Oceania ($5 334.5) in 15.3 times.

The growth of gross national income in the Solomon Islands was 9.1% in the 1970s, ranked 19th in the world, and was on a par with Aruba (9.1%). The growth of GNI in the Solomon Islands (9.1%) was greater than growth of gross national income in the world (4.1%), was greater than growth of GNI in Oceania (2.8%).

Comparison with neighbors. The Solomon Islands gross national income was greater than in Nauru ($30.2 million); but less than in Papua New Guinea ($2.0 billion), in New Caledonia ($685.9 million), and in Vanuatu ($72.6 million). The Solomon Islands gross national income per capita was less than in New Caledonia ($5.4 thousand), in Nauru ($4.3 thousand), in Vanuatu ($736.9), and in Papua New Guinea ($642.1). The growth of gross national income in the Solomon Islands was greater than in Vanuatu (5.7%), in New Caledonia (1.7%), in Papua New Guinea (1.6%), and in Nauru (0.32%).

Comparison with leaders. The Solomon Islands GNI was less than in the United States ($1.7 trillion), in the USSR ($649.4 billion), in Japan ($558.5 billion), in Germany ($486.2 billion), and in France ($334.3 billion). The gross national income per capita in the Solomon Islands was less than in the USA ($7.8 thousand), in France ($6.2 thousand), in Germany ($6.2 thousand), in Japan ($5.0 thousand), and in the USSR ($2.6 thousand). The growth of gross national income in the Solomon Islands was greater than in the USSR (4.8%), in Japan (4.7%), in France (3.9%), in the USA (3.5%), and in Germany (3.0%).

The 1980s

The Solomon Islands gross national income was $153.2 million per year in the 1980s, ranked 164th in the world, and was on a par with the Maldives ($152.1 million). The share in the world was 0.0010%, and 0.061% in Oceania.

The Solomon Islands GNI per capita was $574.4 in the 1980s, ranked 143rd in the world, and was on a par with Indonesia ($587.1). The Solomon Islands gross national income per capita was less than GNI per capita in the world ($3 117.1) in 5.4 times, and was less than GNI per capita in Oceania ($10 137.3) in 17.6 times.

The growth of gross national income in the Solomon Islands was 1.5% in the 1980s, ranked 139th in the world. The growth of GNI in the Solomon Islands (1.5%) was less than growth of GNI in the world (3.0%), was less than growth of GNI in Oceania (2.9%).

Comparison with neighbors. The Solomon Islands GNI was greater than in Vanuatu ($124.8 million) and in Nauru ($42.1 million); but less than in Papua New Guinea ($3.8 billion) and in New Caledonia ($1.2 billion). The Solomon Islands gross national income per capita was less than in New Caledonia ($8.0 thousand), in Nauru ($5.0 thousand), in Vanuatu ($969.0), and in Papua New Guinea ($931.2). The growth of GNI in the Solomon Islands was greater than in Papua New Guinea (1.2%) and in Nauru (-2.8%); but less than in Vanuatu (6.3%) and in New Caledonia (4.5%).

Comparison with leaders. The Solomon Islands GNI was less than in the USA ($4.2 trillion), in Japan ($1.8 trillion), in Germany ($996.5 billion), in the USSR ($887.0 billion), and in France ($732.1 billion). The gross national income per capita in the Solomon Islands was less than in the USA ($17.4 thousand), in Japan ($15.0 thousand), in France ($13.0 thousand), in Germany ($12.8 thousand), and in the USSR ($3.2 thousand). The growth of gross national income in the Solomon Islands was less than in Japan (4.4%), in the USSR (4.3%), in the USA (3.1%), in France (2.3%), and in Germany (2.0%).

The 1990s

The GNI of the Solomon Islands was $316.1 million per year in the 1990s, ranked 189th in the world. The share in the world was 0.0011%, and 0.074% in Oceania.

The gross national income per capita in the Solomon Islands was $889.6 in the 1990s, ranked 141st in the world, and was on a par with Central Asia ($894.8), Indonesia ($907.8). The GNI per capita in the Solomon Islands was less than gross national income per capita in the world ($4 991.4) in 5.6 times, and was less than gross national income per capita in Oceania ($14 867.3) in 16.7 times.

The growth of gross national income in the Solomon Islands was 4.2% in the 1990s, ranked 70th in the world, and was on a par with

Cyprus (4.2%), Guatemala (4.2%), Luxembourg (4.2%). The growth of GNI in the Solomon Islands (4.2%) was greater than growth of gross national income in the world (2.8%), was greater than growth of GNI in Oceania (3.3%).

Comparison with neighbors. The Solomon Islands GNI was greater than in Vanuatu ($223.9 million) and in Nauru ($37.6 million); but less than in Papua New Guinea ($6.4 billion) and in New Caledonia ($3.2 billion). The gross national income per capita in the Solomon Islands was less than in New Caledonia ($16.7 thousand), in Nauru ($3.6 thousand), in Vanuatu ($1 356.4), and in Papua New Guinea ($1 239.5). The growth of gross national income in the Solomon Islands was greater than in Vanuatu (3.0%), in New Caledonia (2.1%), and in Nauru (-10.7%); but less than in Papua New Guinea (6.4%).

Comparison with leaders. The GNI of the Solomon Islands was less than in the United States ($7.5 trillion), in Japan ($4.4 trillion), in Germany ($2.2 trillion), in France ($1.4 trillion), and in the United Kingdom ($1.3 trillion). The Solomon Islands gross national income per capita was less than in Japan ($34.7 thousand), in the USA ($28.5 thousand), in Germany ($27.0 thousand), in France ($24.3 thousand), and in the United Kingdom ($23.0 thousand). The growth of gross national income in the Solomon Islands was greater than in the United States (3.4%), in France (2.2%), in the UK (2.0%), in Germany (2.0%), and in Japan (1.5%).

The 2000s

The Solomon Islands GNI was $408.2 million per year in the 2000s, ranked 197th in the world, and was on a par with Samoa ($410.5 million). The share in the world was 0.0009%, and 0.051% in Oceania.

The gross national income per capita in the Solomon Islands was $879.8 in the 2000s, ranked 169th in the world, and was on a par with Côte d'Ivoire ($893.3), Yemen ($898.7). The GNI per capita in the Solomon Islands was less than gross national income per capita in the world ($7 165.2) in 8.1 times, and was less than GNI per capita in Oceania ($24 025.1) in 27.3 times.

The growth of gross national income in the Solomon Islands was -0.8% in the 2000s, ranked 206th in the world. The growth of gross national income in the Solomon Islands (-0.82%) was less than growth of gross national income in the world (3.0%), was less than growth of GNI in Oceania (2.9%).

Comparison with neighbors. The GNI of the Solomon Islands was greater than in Vanuatu ($387.6 million) and in Nauru ($29.3 million); but less than in Papua New Guinea ($7.1 billion) and in New Caledonia ($6.1 billion). The gross national income per capita in the Solomon Islands was less than in New Caledonia ($26.0 thousand), in Nauru ($2.9 thousand), in Vanuatu ($1 873.0), and in Papua New Guinea ($1 107.3). The growth of gross national income in the Solomon Islands was greater than in Nauru (-1.7%); but less than in Vanuatu (3.4%), in New Caledonia (3.2%), and in Papua New Guinea (1.6%).

Comparison with leaders. The Solomon Islands GNI was less than in the USA ($12.7 trillion), in Japan ($4.8 trillion), in Germany ($2.8 trillion), in China ($2.6 trillion), and in the UK ($2.3 trillion). The Solomon Islands gross national income per capita was less than in the USA ($43.2 thousand), in the United Kingdom ($38.5 thousand), in Japan ($37.1 thousand), in Germany ($34.2 thousand), and in China ($1 950.5). The growth of gross national income in the Solomon Islands was less than in China (10.4%), in the USA (1.8%), in the United Kingdom (1.7%), in Germany (1.0%), and in Japan (0.62%).

The 2010s

The Solomon Islands gross national income was $976.7 million per year in the 2010s, ranked 193rd in the world, and was on a par with Sint Maarten ($967.6 million), the TCI ($987.1 million). The share in the world was 0.0013%, and 0.061% in Oceania.

The Solomon Islands gross national income per capita was $1 637.4 in the 2010s, ranked 168th in the world, and was on a par with Mauritania ($1 639.1), São Tomé and Príncipe ($1 628.2), India ($1 677.9). The Solomon Islands GNI per capita was less than gross national income per capita in the world ($10 611.7) in 6.5 times, and was less than GNI per capita in Oceania ($41 051.4) in 25.1 times.

The growth of gross national income in the Solomon Islands was 7.2% in the 2010s, ranked 9th in the world, and was on a par with Laos (7.2%). The growth of gross national income in the Solomon Islands (7.2%) was greater than growth of GNI in the world (3.1%), was greater than growth of GNI in Oceania (2.7%).

Comparison with neighbors. The GNI of the Solomon Islands was 22.6% higher than in Vanuatu ($796.5 million) and 7.8 times higher than in Nauru ($125.4 million); but 20.9 times lower than in Papua New Guinea ($20.4 billion) and 10.0 times lower than in New Caledonia ($9.7 billion). The gross national income per capita in the Solomon Islands was 22.1 times lower than in New Caledonia ($36.2 thousand), 7.4 times lower than in Nauru ($12.1 thousand), 45.0% lower than in Vanuatu ($3.0 thousand), and 35.6% lower than in Papua New Guinea ($2.5 thousand). The growth of gross national income in the Solomon Islands was greater than in Papua New Guinea (6.0%), in Vanuatu (2.6%), and in New Caledonia (2.4%); but less than in Nauru (12.8%).

Comparison with leaders. The Solomon Islands gross national income was 18 742.6 times lower than in the USA ($18.3 trillion), 10 716.8 times lower than in China ($10.5 trillion), 5 527.7 times lower than in Japan ($5.4 trillion), 3 838.4 times lower than in Germany ($3.7 trillion), and 2 811.6 times lower than in France ($2.7 trillion). The Solomon Islands gross national income per capita was 35.0 times lower than in the USA ($57.3 thousand), 28.0 times lower than in Germany ($45.8 thousand), 25.8 times lower than in Japan ($42.2 thousand), 25.3 times lower than in France ($41.4 thousand), and 4.6 times lower than in China ($7.5 thousand). The growth of GNI in the Solomon Islands was greater than in the USA (2.5%), in Germany (2.0%), in Japan (1.4%), and in France (1.4%); but less than in China (7.7%).

Part II. Structure

	The 2010s
agriculture	26.8%
industry	11.0%
construction	4.4%
trade	21.2%
transportation	5.6%
services	31.1%

Chapter IV. Agriculture

Agriculture, hunting, forestry, fishing (ISIC A-B)

The value of agriculture in the Solomon Islands grew up from $31.2 million per year in the 1970s to $300.5 million per year in the 2010s, that is by $269.3 million or 9.6 times. The change occurred at $195.3 million due to a 2.9-fold increase in prices, as also at $7.5 million due to a 1.1-fold increase in productivity, as well as at $66.5 million due to the growth in population. The average annual growth in agriculture is 3.5%. The minimum value of agriculture was in 1970 at $14.8 million. The maximum value of agriculture was in 2019 at $363.2 million.

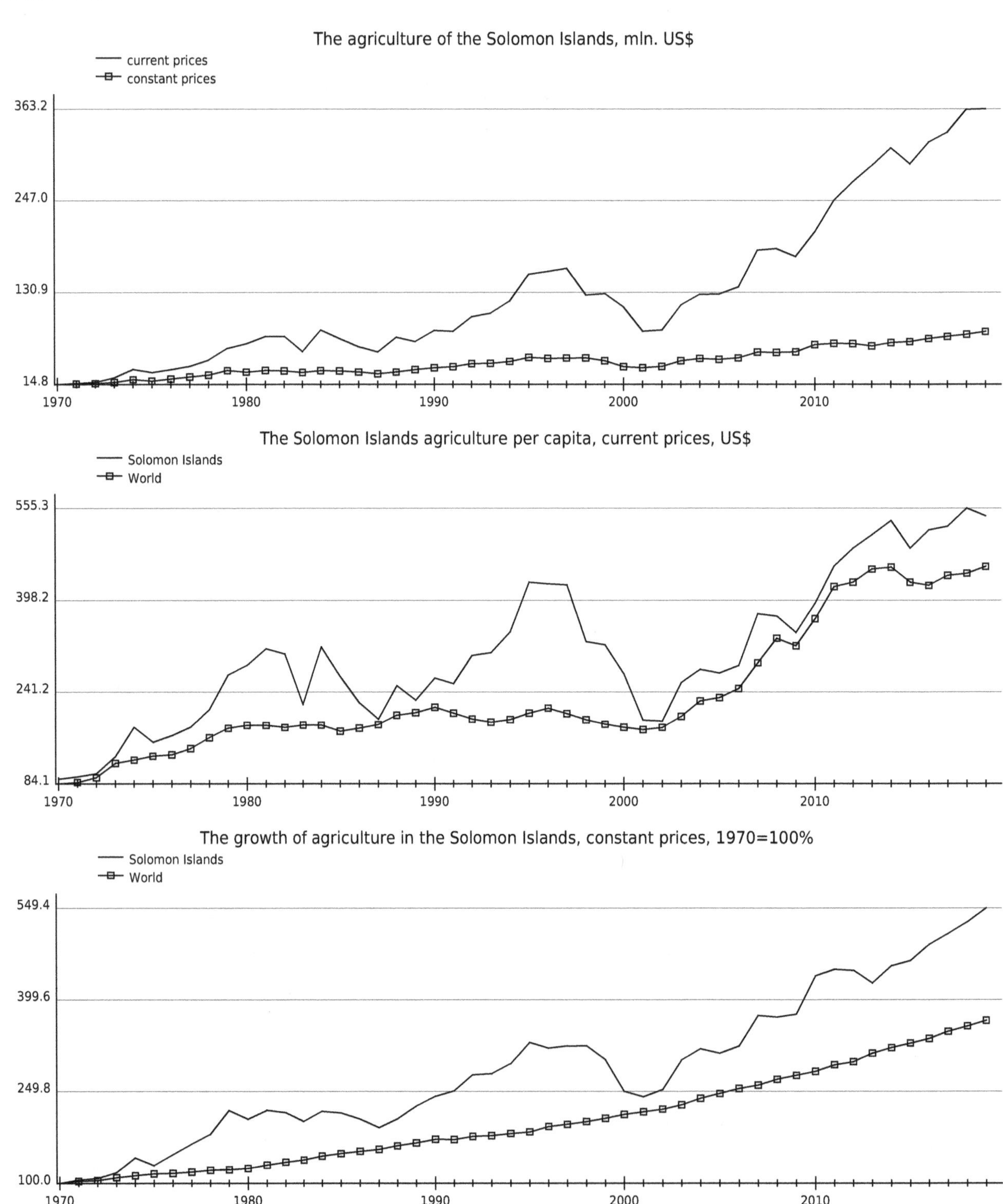

The 1970s

The value added of agriculture in the Solomon Islands was $31.2 million per year in the 1970s, ranked 140th in the world, and was on a par with Lesotho ($31.5 million). The share in the world was 0.0061%, and 0.39% in Oceania.

The share of agriculture in the economy of the Solomon Islands was 51.6% in the 1970s, ranked 7th in the world, and was on a par with Ethiopia (51.5%).

The value of agriculture per capita in the Solomon Islands was $163.8 in the 1970s, ranked 53rd in the world, and was on a par with São Tomé and Príncipe ($161.8), Melanesia ($167.3), Tonga ($167.9). The sector of agriculture per capita in the Solomon Islands was greater than agriculture per capita in the world ($127.6) by 28.3%, and was less than agriculture per capita in Oceania ($377.5) in 2.3 times.

The growth of agriculture in the Solomon Islands was 9.1% in the 1970s, ranked 8th in the world, and was on a par with Aruba (9.1%), the Netherlands (9.1%). The growth of agriculture in the Solomon Islands (9.1%) was greater than growth of agriculture in the world (2.2%), was greater than growth of agriculture in Oceania (2.4%).

Comparison with neighbors. The agriculture of the Solomon Islands was greater than in New Caledonia ($23.8 million), in Vanuatu ($22.0 million), and in Nauru ($1.9 million); but less than in Papua New Guinea ($478.3 million). The Solomon Islands agriculture per capita was greater than in Papua New Guinea ($153.7); but less than in Nauru ($271.0), in Vanuatu ($223.4), and in New Caledonia ($188.3). The growth of agriculture in the Solomon Islands was greater than in Vanuatu (7.7%), in Papua New Guinea (2.7%), in Nauru (1.1%), and in New Caledonia (-2.7%).

Comparison with leaders. The Solomon Islands agriculture was less than in the USSR ($88.7 billion), in China ($49.5 billion), in the USA ($42.6 billion), in India ($36.0 billion), and in Japan ($25.8 billion). The sector of agriculture per capita in the Solomon Islands was greater than in India ($58.3) and in China ($54.2); but less than in the USSR ($351.8), in Japan ($231.3), and in the United States ($195.0). The growth of agriculture in the Solomon Islands was greater than in the USSR (7.0%), in China (2.4%), in Japan (0.52%), in the USA (0.34%), and in India (0.30%).

The 1980s

The value of agriculture in the Solomon Islands was $69.0 million per year in the 1980s, ranked 142nd in the world. The share in the world was 0.0076%, and 0.51% in Oceania.

The share of agriculture in the economy of the Solomon Islands was 49.7% in the 1980s, ranked 7th in the world, and was on a par with Rwanda (49.8%).

The sector of agriculture per capita in the Solomon Islands was $258.6 in the 1980s, ranked 58th in the world, and was on a par with Poland ($259.1), Bulgaria ($257.0), Ivory Coast ($256.0). The agriculture per capita in the Solomon Islands was greater than agriculture per capita in the world ($186.6) by 38.6%, and was less than agriculture per capita in Oceania ($545.9) in 2.1 times.

The growth of agriculture in the Solomon Islands was 0.3% in the 1980s, ranked 149th in the world. The growth of agriculture in the Solomon Islands (0.32%) was less than growth of agriculture in the world (3.1%), was less than growth of agriculture in Oceania (2.0%).

Comparison with neighbors. The sector of agriculture in the Solomon Islands was greater than in Vanuatu ($37.0 million), in New Caledonia ($23.4 million), and in Nauru ($2.6 million); but less than in Papua New Guinea ($893.1 million). The value of agriculture per capita in the Solomon Islands was greater than in Papua New Guinea ($221.5) and in New Caledonia ($150.6); but less than in Nauru ($308.7) and in Vanuatu ($287.4). The growth of agriculture in the Solomon Islands was greater than in New Caledonia (-0.49%) and in Nauru (-2.4%); but less than in Papua New Guinea (2.4%) and in Vanuatu (0.76%).

Comparison with leaders. The agriculture of the Solomon Islands was less than in the USSR ($125.8 billion), in China ($94.9 billion), in India ($70.4 billion), in the United States ($68.7 billion), and in Japan ($49.7 billion). The Solomon Islands agriculture per capita was greater than in India ($90.7) and in China ($88.5); but less than in the USSR ($457.2), in Japan ($410.0), and in the United States ($286.8). The growth of agriculture in the Solomon Islands was less than in China (5.3%), in India (4.4%), in the United States (3.7%), in the USSR (2.8%), and in Japan (0.41%).

The 1990s

The Solomon Islands agriculture was $122.0 million per year in the 1990s, ranked 161st in the world, and was on a par with Eritrea ($124.2 million). The share in the world was 0.011%, and 0.69% in Oceania.

The share of agriculture in the economy of the Solomon Islands was 41.8% in the 1990s, ranked 13th in the world, and was on a par with Laos (41.4%), Uzbekistan (42.2%).

The value of agriculture per capita in the Solomon Islands was $343.3 in the 1990s, ranked 50th in the world, and was on a par with Georgia ($343.7), Gabon ($347.7), Saint Lucia ($338.0). The Solomon Islands agriculture per capita was greater than agriculture per capita in the world ($199.8) by 71.8%, and was less than agriculture per capita in Oceania ($608.8) by 43.6%.

The growth of agriculture in the Solomon Islands was 2.9% in the 1990s, ranked 75th in the world. The growth of agriculture in the Solomon Islands (2.9%) was greater than growth of agriculture in the world (2.2%), was less than growth of agriculture in Oceania (3.7%).

Comparison with neighbors. The Solomon Islands agriculture was greater than in Vanuatu ($62.5 million), in New Caledonia ($61.1 million), and in Nauru ($2.4 million); but less than in Papua New Guinea ($1.3 billion). The value of agriculture per capita in the Solomon Islands was greater than in New Caledonia ($319.9), in Papua New Guinea ($257.9), and in Nauru ($234.2); but less than in Vanuatu ($378.9). The growth of agriculture in the Solomon Islands was greater than in Nauru (-13.3%); but less than in Vanuatu (5.9%), in Papua New Guinea (4.5%), and in New Caledonia (4.2%).

Comparison with leaders. The value of agriculture in the Solomon Islands was less than in China ($139.0 billion), in the United States ($96.1 billion), in India ($91.4 billion), in Japan ($78.9 billion), and in Brazil ($36.8 billion). The value of agriculture per capita in the Solomon Islands was greater than in Brazil ($228.7), in China ($112.7), and in India ($95.6); but less than in Japan ($625.5) and in the United States ($363.4). The growth of agriculture in the Solomon Islands was greater than in India (2.8%), in the United States (2.6%), and in Japan (-1.8%); but less than in China (4.3%) and in Brazil (3.0%).

The 2000s

The value of agriculture in the Solomon Islands was $133.4 million per year in the 2000s, ranked 164th in the world, and was on a par with Hong Kong ($132.7 million). The share in the world was 0.0085%, and 0.50% in Oceania.

The share of agriculture in the economy of the Solomon Islands was 30.7% in the 2000s, ranked 22nd in the world.

The Solomon Islands agriculture per capita was $287.5 in the 2000s, ranked 75th in the world, and was on a par with Panama ($287.0), Ghana ($288.6), Latvia ($285.6). The sector of agriculture per capita in the Solomon Islands was greater than agriculture per capita in the world ($240.3) by 19.6%, and was less than agriculture per capita in Oceania ($806.4) in 2.8 times.

The growth of agriculture in the Solomon Islands was 2.2% in the 2000s, ranked 97th in the world, and was on a par with Finland (2.2%), Vanuatu (2.2%), Madagascar (2.3%). The growth of agriculture in the Solomon Islands (2.2%) was less than growth of agriculture in the world (3.0%), was greater than growth of agriculture in Oceania (1.5%).

Comparison with neighbors. The sector of agriculture in the Solomon Islands was greater than in New Caledonia ($99.1 million), in Vanuatu ($87.9 million), and in Nauru ($1.9 million); but less than in Papua New Guinea ($1.6 billion). The Solomon Islands agriculture per capita was greater than in Papua New Guinea ($248.4) and in Nauru ($186.5); but less than in Vanuatu ($424.6) and in New Caledonia ($422.9). The growth of agriculture in the Solomon Islands was greater than in Vanuatu (2.2%), in Papua New Guinea

(1.6%), in New Caledonia (-1.8%), and in Nauru (-4.3%).

Comparison with leaders. The value of agriculture in the Solomon Islands was less than in China ($297.7 billion), in India ($147.6 billion), in the USA ($122.5 billion), in Japan ($57.1 billion), and in Nigeria ($47.6 billion). The Solomon Islands agriculture per capita was greater than in China ($224.5) and in India ($129.7); but less than in Japan ($445.6), in the United States ($416.9), and in Nigeria ($346.4). The growth of agriculture in the Solomon Islands was greater than in India (2.0%) and in Japan (-1.3%); but less than in Nigeria (10.1%), in China (4.0%), and in the United States (3.6%).

The 2010s

The agriculture of the Solomon Islands was $300.5 million per year in the 2010s, ranked 159th in the world, and was on a par with Bhutan ($300.0 million). The share in the world was 0.0095%, and 0.62% in Oceania.

The share of agriculture in the economy of the Solomon Islands was 26.8% in the 2010s, ranked 26th in the world, and was on a par with Myanmar (27.0%), Rwanda (27.0%).

The value added of agriculture per capita in the Solomon Islands was $503.7 in the 2010s, ranked 58th in the world, and was on a par with the Americas ($498.8), South America ($511.1), the Cook Islands ($511.8). The sector of agriculture per capita in the Solomon Islands was greater than agriculture per capita in the world ($432.1) by 16.6%, and was less than agriculture per capita in Oceania ($1 242.3) in 2.5 times.

The growth of agriculture in the Solomon Islands was 3.9% in the 2010s, ranked 44th in the world, and was on a par with Indonesia (3.9%), Sierra Leone (3.9%). The growth of agriculture in the Solomon Islands (3.9%) was greater than growth of agriculture in the world (2.9%), was greater than growth of agriculture in Oceania (-0.30%).

Comparison with neighbors. The Solomon Islands agriculture was 63.8% higher than in Vanuatu ($183.4 million), 81.8% higher than in New Caledonia ($165.3 million), and 103.8 times higher than in Nauru ($2.9 million); but 12.8 times lower than in Papua New Guinea ($3.9 billion). The value of agriculture per capita in the Solomon Islands was 5.0% higher than in Papua New Guinea ($479.9) and 80.2% higher than in Nauru ($279.5); but 26.5% lower than in Vanuatu ($685.4) and 18.1% lower than in New Caledonia ($614.9). The growth of agriculture in the Solomon Islands was greater than in Papua New Guinea (2.6%) and in Vanuatu (1.6%); but less than in New Caledonia (9.6%) and in Nauru (4.6%).

Comparison with leaders. The value added of agriculture in the Solomon Islands was 2 949.5 times lower than in China ($886.2 billion), 1 209.5 times lower than in India ($363.4 billion), 600.0 times lower than in the United States ($180.3 billion), 412.9 times lower than in Indonesia ($124.1 billion), and 318.7 times lower than in Nigeria ($95.8 billion). The agriculture per capita in the Solomon Islands was 4.2% higher than in Indonesia ($483.6) and 80.4% higher than in India ($279.1); but 20.3% lower than in China ($631.9), 10.7% lower than in the United States ($564.3), and 5.8% lower than in Nigeria ($534.6). The growth of agriculture in the Solomon Islands was greater than in Indonesia (3.9%), in China (3.8%), in Nigeria (3.6%), and in the United States (2.0%); but less than in India (4.1%).

Chapter V. Industry

Mining, Manufacturing, Utilities (ISIC C-E)

The Solomon Islands industry increased from $2.6 million per year in the 1970s to $123.0 million per year in the 2010s, that is by $120.4 million or 47.9 times. The change occurred at $101.2 million due to a 5.6-fold increase in prices, as also at $13.7 million due to a 2.7-fold increase in productivity, as well as at $5.5 million due to the increase in population. The average annual growth in industry is 5.3%. The minimum value of industry was in 1970 at $1.2 million. The maximum value of industry was in 2017 at $142.3 million.

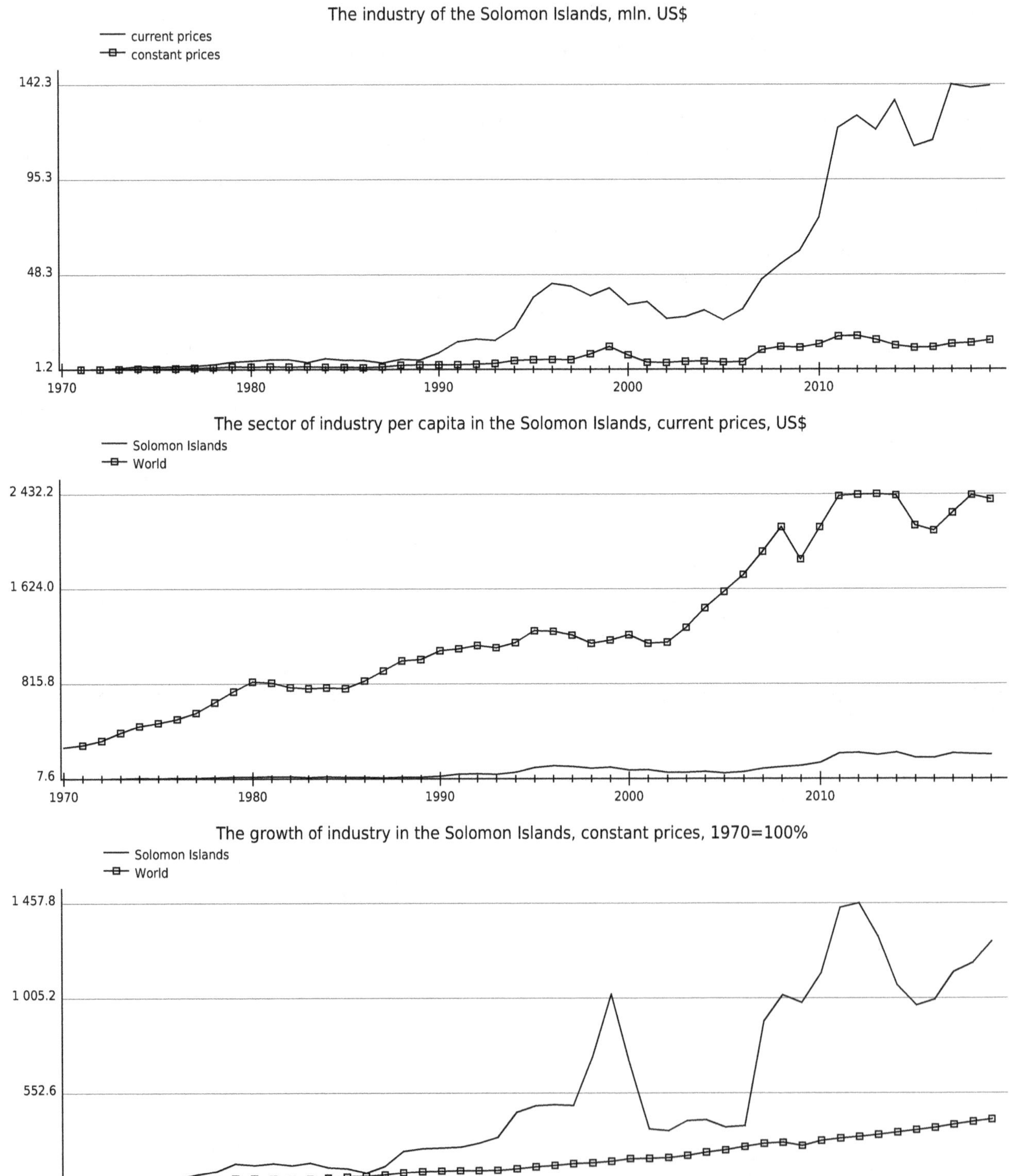

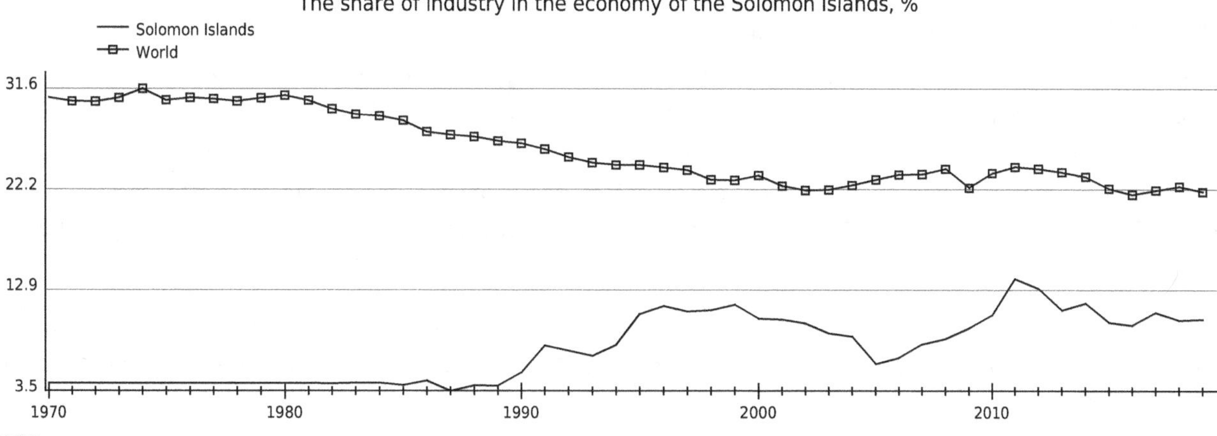

The share of industry in the economy of the Solomon Islands, %

The 1970s

The industry of the Solomon Islands was $2.6 million per year in the 1970s, ranked 172nd in the world, and was on a par with Tonga ($2.6 million). The share in the world was 0.0001%, and 0.0085% in Oceania.

The share of industry in the economy of the Solomon Islands was 4.2% in the 1970s, ranked 179th in the world.

The Solomon Islands industry per capita was $13.5 in the 1970s, ranked 173rd in the world, and was on a par with Rwanda ($13.5). The value of industry per capita in the Solomon Islands was less than industry per capita in the world ($480.5) in 35.6 times, and was less than industry per capita in Oceania ($1 413.2) in 104.8 times.

The growth of industry in the Solomon Islands was 9% in the 1970s, ranked 25th in the world, and was on a par with China (8.9%). The growth of industry in the Solomon Islands (9.0%) was greater than growth of industry in the world (4.0%), was greater than growth of industry in Oceania (3.0%).

Comparison with neighbors. The industry of the Solomon Islands was less than in Papua New Guinea ($376.8 million), in New Caledonia ($211.6 million), in Nauru ($8.4 million), and in Vanuatu ($3.9 million). The sector of industry per capita in the Solomon Islands was less than in New Caledonia ($1 677.9), in Nauru ($1 178.5), in Papua New Guinea ($121.1), and in Vanuatu ($39.9). The growth of industry in the Solomon Islands was greater than in Vanuatu (7.7%), in Papua New Guinea (2.7%), in Nauru (-1.2%), and in New Caledonia (-2.0%).

Comparison with leaders. The Solomon Islands industry was less than in the USA ($450.4 billion), in the USSR ($248.8 billion), in Japan ($185.6 billion), in Germany ($158.4 billion), and in the UK ($72.6 billion). The industry per capita in the Solomon Islands was less than in the United States ($2.1 thousand), in Germany ($2.0 thousand), in Japan ($1 666.5), in the UK ($1 295.1), and in the USSR ($986.6). The growth of industry in the Solomon Islands was greater than in the USSR (5.2%), in Japan (4.5%), in the USA (2.4%), in Germany (2.1%), and in the United Kingdom (1.9%).

The 1980s

The value added of industry in the Solomon Islands was $5.8 million per year in the 1980s, ranked 175th in the world. The share in the world was 0.0001%, and 0.0090% in Oceania.

The share of industry in the economy of the Solomon Islands was 4.1% in the 1980s, ranked 180th in the world.

The value added of industry per capita in the Solomon Islands was $21.6 in the 1980s, ranked 176th in the world. The value of industry per capita in the Solomon Islands was less than industry per capita in the world ($861.8) in 40.0 times, and was less than industry per capita in Oceania ($2 572.3) in 119.2 times.

The growth of industry in the Solomon Islands was 2.9% in the 1980s, ranked 93rd in the world, and was on a par with the Caribbean (2.9%), Oceania (2.9%), the FSM (2.9%). The growth of industry in the Solomon Islands (2.9%) was greater than growth of industry in the world (2.3%), was less than growth of industry in Oceania (2.9%).

Comparison with neighbors. The sector of industry in the Solomon Islands was less than in Papua New Guinea ($673.2 million), in New Caledonia ($287.8 million), in Nauru ($12.5 million), and in Vanuatu ($6.9 million). The value added of industry per capita in the Solomon Islands was less than in New Caledonia ($1 852.7), in Nauru ($1 475.4), in Papua New Guinea ($167.0), and in Vanuatu

($53.6). The growth of industry in the Solomon Islands was greater than in Papua New Guinea (-1.5%) and in Nauru (-3.9%); but less than in Vanuatu (7.3%) and in New Caledonia (6.9%).

Comparison with leaders. The value of industry in the Solomon Islands was less than in the United States ($1.0 trillion), in Japan ($566.4 billion), in the USSR ($305.7 billion), in Germany ($297.5 billion), and in the UK ($171.2 billion). The sector of industry per capita in the Solomon Islands was less than in Japan ($4.7 thousand), in the United States ($4.2 thousand), in Germany ($3.8 thousand), in the United Kingdom ($3.0 thousand), and in the USSR ($1 110.8). The growth of industry in the Solomon Islands was greater than in the USA (1.9%), in the UK (1.4%), and in Germany (1.2%); but less than in the USSR (5.3%) and in Japan (4.2%).

The 1990s

The value added of industry in the Solomon Islands was $28.0 million per year in the 1990s, ranked 190th in the world, and was on a par with Samoa ($27.8 million), Grenada ($28.2 million), Dominica ($27.5 million). The share in the world was 0.0004%, and 0.031% in Oceania.

The share of industry in the economy of the Solomon Islands was 9.6% in the 1990s, ranked 176th in the world, and was on a par with Polynesia (9.6%).

The value of industry per capita in the Solomon Islands was $78.7 in the 1990s, ranked 172nd in the world, and was on a par with São Tomé and Príncipe ($78.5). The value of industry per capita in the Solomon Islands was less than industry per capita in the world ($1 175.6) in 14.9 times, and was less than industry per capita in Oceania ($3 075.6) in 39.1 times.

The growth of industry in the Solomon Islands was 13.5% in the 1990s, ranked 4th in the world, and was on a par with Vietnam (13.4%). The growth of industry in the Solomon Islands (13.5%) was greater than growth of industry in the world (2.5%), was greater than growth of industry in Oceania (2.3%).

Comparison with neighbors. The sector of industry in the Solomon Islands was greater than in Vanuatu ($15.5 million) and in Nauru ($10.3 million); but less than in Papua New Guinea ($1.4 billion) and in New Caledonia ($501.8 million). The industry per capita in the Solomon Islands was less than in New Caledonia ($2.6 thousand), in Nauru ($995.1), in Papua New Guinea ($271.3), and in Vanuatu ($93.7). The growth of industry in the Solomon Islands was greater than in Papua New Guinea (11.9%), in Vanuatu (2.0%), in New Caledonia (-6.1%), and in Nauru (-6.3%).

Comparison with leaders. The Solomon Islands industry was less than in the United States ($1.5 trillion), in Japan ($1.2 trillion), in Germany ($534.0 billion), in China ($285.9 billion), and in the UK ($268.6 billion). The industry per capita in the Solomon Islands was less than in Japan ($9.4 thousand), in Germany ($6.6 thousand), in the United States ($5.7 thousand), in the UK ($4.6 thousand), and in China ($231.9). The growth of industry in the Solomon Islands was greater than in China (13.1%), in the United States (2.8%), in Japan (1.3%), in the United Kingdom (1.2%), and in Germany (0.33%).

The 2000s

The value added of industry in the Solomon Islands was $36.8 million per year in the 2000s, ranked 196th in the world, and was on a par with the TCI ($37.1 million), Dominica ($37.3 million). The share in the world was 0.0004%, and 0.024% in Oceania.

The share of industry in the economy of the Solomon Islands was 8.4% in the 2000s, ranked 180th in the world.

The Solomon Islands industry per capita was $79.2 in the 2000s, ranked 180th in the world, and was on a par with Tajikistan ($79.0), Burkina Faso ($78.7), Mali ($79.9). The Solomon Islands industry per capita was less than industry per capita in the world ($1 573.8) in 19.9 times, and was less than industry per capita in Oceania ($4 570.1) in 57.7 times.

The growth of industry in the Solomon Islands was -0.4% in the 2000s, ranked 183rd in the world, and was on a par with Hong Kong (-0.42%). The growth of industry in the Solomon Islands (-0.41%) was less than growth of industry in the world (2.9%), was less than growth of industry in Oceania (1.8%).

Comparison with neighbors. The industry of the Solomon Islands was greater than in Vanuatu ($21.8 million) and in Nauru ($8.2 million); but less than in Papua New Guinea ($2.0 billion) and in New Caledonia ($973.2 million). The sector of industry per capita in the Solomon Islands was less than in New Caledonia ($4.2 thousand), in Nauru ($820.0), in Papua New Guinea ($303.7), and in Vanuatu ($105.3). The growth of industry in the Solomon Islands was greater than in Papua New Guinea (-0.84%); but less than in New Caledonia (1.4%), in Vanuatu (1.0%), and in Nauru (0.23%).

Comparison with leaders. The industry of the Solomon Islands was less than in the USA ($2.1 trillion), in Japan ($1.1 trillion), in China ($1.1 trillion), in Germany ($629.4 billion), and in the UK ($345.1 billion). The Solomon Islands industry per capita was less than in Japan ($8.8 thousand), in Germany ($7.7 thousand), in the USA ($7.1 thousand), in the UK ($5.7 thousand), and in China ($795.3). The growth of industry in the Solomon Islands was greater than in the UK (-1.1%); but less than in China (11.1%), in the United States (1.5%), in Germany (0.19%), and in Japan (0.15%).

The 2010s

The industry of the Solomon Islands was $123.0 million per year in the 2010s, ranked 184th in the world. The share in the world was 0.0007%, and 0.044% in Oceania.

The share of industry in the economy of the Solomon Islands was 11.0% in the 2010s, ranked 161st in the world.

The value added of industry per capita in the Solomon Islands was $206.1 in the 2010s, ranked 176th in the world, and was on a par with Cambodia ($209.6). The Solomon Islands industry per capita was less than industry per capita in the world ($2 320.9) in 11.3 times, and was less than industry per capita in Oceania ($7 127.9) in 34.6 times.

The growth of industry in the Solomon Islands was 2.7% in the 2010s, ranked 101st in the world, and was on a par with Saudi Arabia (2.6%), Thailand (2.6%), Liberia (2.6%). The growth of industry in the Solomon Islands (2.7%) was less than growth of industry in the world (3.5%), was greater than growth of industry in Oceania (2.6%).

Comparison with neighbors. The value added of industry in the Solomon Islands was 2.9 times higher than in Vanuatu ($43.1 million) and 2.9 times higher than in Nauru ($41.8 million); but 43.0 times lower than in Papua New Guinea ($5.3 billion) and 9.6 times lower than in New Caledonia ($1.2 billion). The Solomon Islands industry per capita was 28.0% higher than in Vanuatu ($161.0); but 21.3 times lower than in New Caledonia ($4.4 thousand), 19.6 times lower than in Nauru ($4.0 thousand), and 3.2 times lower than in Papua New Guinea ($657.8). The growth of industry in the Solomon Islands was greater than in New Caledonia (1.9%); but less than in Papua New Guinea (10.2%), in Nauru (6.7%), and in Vanuatu (3.3%).

Comparison with leaders. The Solomon Islands industry was 29 952.9 times lower than in China ($3.7 trillion), 22 296.0 times lower than in the USA ($2.7 trillion), 9 680.8 times lower than in Japan ($1.2 trillion), 6 830.9 times lower than in Germany ($840.0 billion), and 3 605.7 times lower than in India ($443.4 billion). The Solomon Islands industry per capita was 49.8 times lower than in Germany ($10.3 thousand), 45.1 times lower than in Japan ($9.3 thousand), 41.6 times lower than in the United States ($8.6 thousand), 12.7 times lower than in China ($2.6 thousand), and 39.5% lower than in India ($340.6). The growth of industry in the Solomon Islands was greater than in Japan (2.6%) and in the USA (2.2%); but less than in China (7.5%), in India (6.5%), and in Germany (3.2%).

Chapter 5.1. Manufacturing

(ISIC D)

The value added of manufacturing in the Solomon Islands grew up from $2.3 million per year in the 1970s to $91.8 million per year in the 2010s, that is by $89.5 million or 39.8 times. The change occurred at $75.0 million due to a 5.5-fold increase in prices, as also at $9.6 million due to a 2.3-fold increase in productivity, as well as at $4.9 million due to the rise in population. The average annual growth in manufacturing is 5.3%. The minimum value of manufacturing was in 1970 at $1.1 million. The maximum value of manufacturing was in 2017 at $120.8 million.

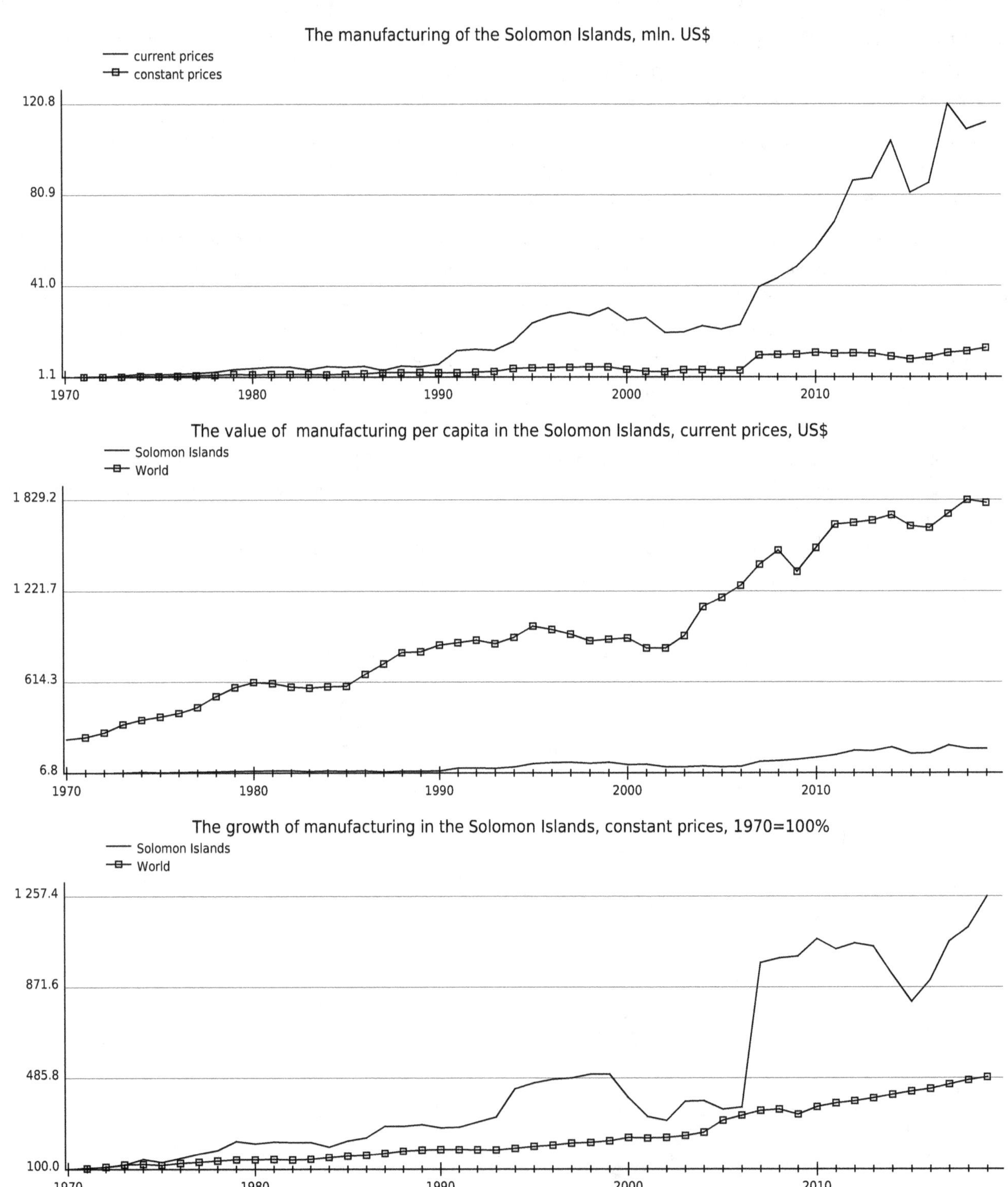

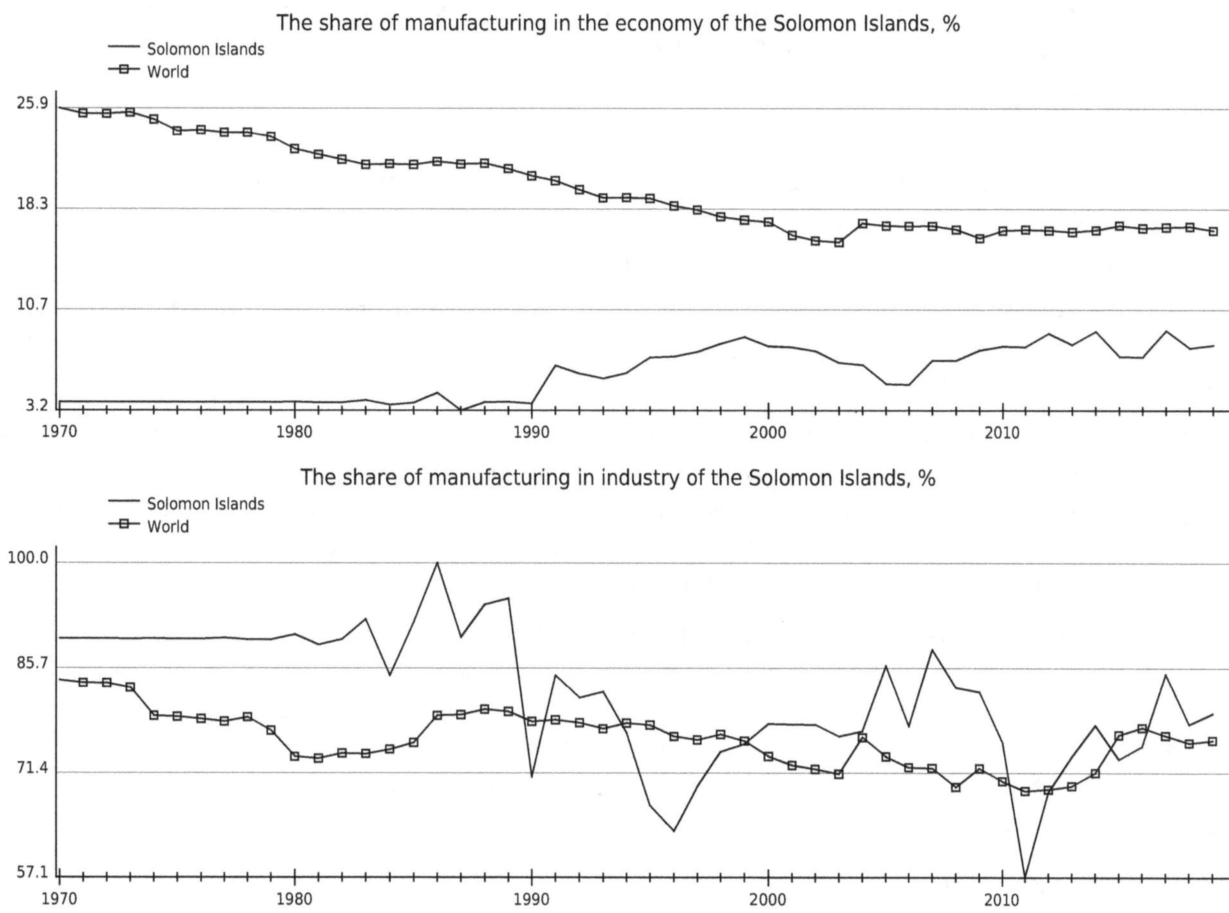

The 1970s

The value added of manufacturing in the Solomon Islands was $2.3 million per year in the 1970s, ranked 166th in the world. The share in the world was 0.0001%, and 0.011% in Oceania.

The share of manufacturing in the economy of the Solomon Islands was 3.8% in the 1970s, ranked 162nd in the world, and was on a par with Grenada (3.8%).

The manufacturing per capita in the Solomon Islands was $12.1 in the 1970s, ranked 166th in the world. The Solomon Islands manufacturing per capita was less than manufacturing per capita in the world ($383.2) in 31.7 times, and was less than manufacturing per capita in Oceania ($1 020.6) in 84.4 times.

The growth of manufacturing in the Solomon Islands was 9% in the 1970s, ranked 26th in the world, and was on a par with Western Africa (9.1%), Aruba (9.1%). The growth of manufacturing in the Solomon Islands (9.0%) was greater than growth of manufacturing in the world (3.8%), was greater than growth of manufacturing in Oceania (2.1%).

Comparison with neighbors. The value of manufacturing in the Solomon Islands was greater than in Nauru ($548.5 thousand); but less than in New Caledonia ($195.4 million), in Papua New Guinea ($77.9 million), and in Vanuatu ($2.8 million). The manufacturing per capita in the Solomon Islands was less than in New Caledonia ($1 549.4), in Nauru ($77.3), in Vanuatu ($27.9), and in Papua New Guinea ($25.0). The growth of manufacturing in the Solomon Islands was greater than in Vanuatu (7.7%), in Papua New Guinea (2.9%), in Nauru (1.1%), and in New Caledonia (-2.6%).

Comparison with leaders. The sector of manufacturing in the Solomon Islands was less than in the USA ($378.0 billion), in the USSR ($248.8 billion), in Japan ($169.3 billion), in Germany ($138.0 billion), and in France ($64.5 billion). The value of manufacturing per capita in the Solomon Islands was less than in Germany ($1 752.1), in the USA ($1 731.8), in Japan ($1 520.6), in France ($1 203.0), and in the USSR ($986.6). The growth of manufacturing in the Solomon Islands was greater than in the USSR (5.2%), in Japan (4.5%), in France (3.5%), in the USA (2.7%), and in Germany (2.1%).

The 1980s

The manufacturing of the Solomon Islands was $5.3 million per year in the 1980s, ranked 171st in the world, and was on a par with Tonga ($5.4 million). The share in the world was 0.0002%, and 0.013% in Oceania.

The share of manufacturing in the economy of the Solomon Islands was 3.8% in the 1980s, ranked 167th in the world, and was on a par with Laos (3.8%).

The manufacturing per capita in the Solomon Islands was $19.8 in the 1980s, ranked 170th in the world, and was on a par with Micronesia ($20.3). The value of manufacturing per capita in the Solomon Islands was less than manufacturing per capita in the world ($661.2) in 33.4 times, and was less than manufacturing per capita in Oceania ($1 656.8) in 83.8 times.

The growth of manufacturing in the Solomon Islands was 2.8% in the 1980s, ranked 96th in the world. The growth of manufacturing in the Solomon Islands (2.8%) was greater than growth of manufacturing in the world (2.6%), was greater than growth of manufacturing in Oceania (1.5%).

Comparison with neighbors. The manufacturing of the Solomon Islands was greater than in Vanuatu ($4.8 million) and in Nauru ($743.7 thousand); but less than in New Caledonia ($258.2 million) and in Papua New Guinea ($179.8 million). The sector of manufacturing per capita in the Solomon Islands was less than in New Caledonia ($1 662.4), in Nauru ($88.0), in Papua New Guinea ($44.6), and in Vanuatu ($37.6). The growth of manufacturing in the Solomon Islands was greater than in Papua New Guinea (0.42%) and in Nauru (-2.4%); but less than in Vanuatu (8.5%) and in New Caledonia (7.1%).

Comparison with leaders. The value of manufacturing in the Solomon Islands was less than in the United States ($789.4 billion), in Japan ($501.0 billion), in the USSR ($305.7 billion), in Germany ($258.7 billion), and in Italy ($134.1 billion). The value of manufacturing per capita in the Solomon Islands was less than in Japan ($4.1 thousand), in Germany ($3.3 thousand), in the USA ($3.3 thousand), in Italy ($2.4 thousand), and in the USSR ($1 110.8). The growth of manufacturing in the Solomon Islands was greater than in Italy (2.5%), in the USA (1.9%), and in Germany (1.2%); but less than in the USSR (5.3%) and in Japan (4.4%).

The 1990s

The value of manufacturing in the Solomon Islands was $20.3 million per year in the 1990s, ranked 187th in the world, and was on a par with Liberia ($20.4 million), Saint Kitts and Nevis ($20.7 million). The share in the world was 0.0004%, and 0.035% in Oceania.

The share of manufacturing in the economy of the Solomon Islands was 7.0% in the 1990s, ranked 163rd in the world.

The Solomon Islands manufacturing per capita was $57.1 in the 1990s, ranked 165th in the world, and was on a par with Pakistan ($57.6), Albania ($55.9). The manufacturing per capita in the Solomon Islands was less than manufacturing per capita in the world ($908.4) in 15.9 times, and was less than manufacturing per capita in Oceania ($1 986.6) in 34.8 times.

The growth of manufacturing in the Solomon Islands was 5.7% in the 1990s, ranked 43rd in the world, and was on a par with Palestine (5.7%), San Marino (5.7%), Gabon (5.7%). The growth of manufacturing in the Solomon Islands (5.7%) was greater than growth of manufacturing in the world (2.0%), was greater than growth of manufacturing in Oceania (1.3%).

Comparison with neighbors. The manufacturing of the Solomon Islands was greater than in Vanuatu ($11.2 million) and in Nauru ($688.7 thousand); but less than in New Caledonia ($436.9 million) and in Papua New Guinea ($236.2 million). The Solomon Islands manufacturing per capita was greater than in Papua New Guinea ($45.9); but less than in New Caledonia ($2.3 thousand), in Vanuatu ($67.8), and in Nauru ($66.8). The growth of manufacturing in the Solomon Islands was greater than in Papua New Guinea (2.3%), in Vanuatu (2.0%), in New Caledonia (-7.0%), and in Nauru (-12.7%).

Comparison with leaders. The value of manufacturing in the Solomon Islands was less than in the United States ($1.2 trillion), in Japan ($1.0 trillion), in Germany ($468.8 billion), in Italy ($227.8 billion), and in France ($215.0 billion). The value added of manufacturing per capita in the Solomon Islands was less than in Japan ($8.3 thousand), in Germany ($5.8 thousand), in the USA ($4.7 thousand), in Italy ($4.0 thousand), and in France ($3.6 thousand). The growth of manufacturing in the Solomon Islands was greater than in the USA (3.2%), in France (2.4%), in Italy (1.2%), in Japan (1.1%), and in Germany (0.26%).

The 2000s

The value of manufacturing in the Solomon Islands was $29.8 million per year in the 2000s, ranked 189th in the world. The share in the world was 0.0004%, and 0.036% in Oceania.

The share of manufacturing in the economy of the Solomon Islands was 6.8% in the 2000s, ranked 160th in the world, and was on a par with Niger (6.8%), São Tomé and Príncipe (6.9%), Greenland (6.9%).

The value added of manufacturing per capita in the Solomon Islands was $64.2 in the 2000s, ranked 174th in the world, and was on a par with Burkina Faso ($62.9). The manufacturing per capita in the Solomon Islands was less than manufacturing per capita in the world ($1 138.1) in 17.7 times, and was less than manufacturing per capita in Oceania ($2 480.4) in 38.6 times.

The growth of manufacturing in the Solomon Islands was 7.1% in the 2000s, ranked 33rd in the world, and was on a par with Rwanda (7.2%). The growth of manufacturing in the Solomon Islands (7.1%) was greater than growth of manufacturing in the world (4.2%), was greater than growth of manufacturing in Oceania (0.79%).

Comparison with neighbors. The Solomon Islands manufacturing was greater than in Vanuatu ($14.1 million) and in Nauru ($2.7 million); but less than in New Caledonia ($876.2 million) and in Papua New Guinea ($190.5 million). The value of manufacturing per capita in the Solomon Islands was greater than in Papua New Guinea ($29.5); but less than in New Caledonia ($3.7 thousand), in Nauru ($270.9), and in Vanuatu ($68.3). The growth of manufacturing in the Solomon Islands was greater than in New Caledonia (1.7%), in Papua New Guinea (1.7%), and in Vanuatu (-1.3%); but less than in Nauru (29.2%).

Comparison with leaders. The value added of manufacturing in the Solomon Islands was less than in the USA ($1.6 trillion), in China ($1.1 trillion), in Japan ($992.9 billion), in Germany ($551.4 billion), and in Italy ($277.2 billion). The value added of manufacturing per capita in the Solomon Islands was less than in Japan ($7.7 thousand), in Germany ($6.8 thousand), in the USA ($5.6 thousand), in Italy ($4.8 thousand), and in China ($815.3). The growth of manufacturing in the Solomon Islands was greater than in the United States (1.6%), in Japan (0.32%), in Germany (0.097%), and in Italy (-1.3%).

The 2010s

The value of manufacturing in the Solomon Islands was $91.8 million per year in the 2010s, ranked 179th in the world, and was on a par with the Seychelles ($89.6 million). The share in the world was 0.0007%, and 0.082% in Oceania.

The share of manufacturing in the economy of the Solomon Islands was 8.2% in the 2010s, ranked 141st in the world, and was on a par with Samoa (8.2%).

The value added of manufacturing per capita in the Solomon Islands was $153.9 in the 2010s, ranked 164th in the world. The value added of manufacturing per capita in the Solomon Islands was less than manufacturing per capita in the world ($1 697.4) in 11.0 times, and was less than manufacturing per capita in Oceania ($2 847.4) in 18.5 times.

The growth of manufacturing in the Solomon Islands was 2.3% in the 2010s, ranked 126th in the world, and was on a par with the Netherlands (2.3%), Namibia (2.3%), Northern Africa (2.3%). The growth of manufacturing in the Solomon Islands (2.3%) was less than growth of manufacturing in the world (3.9%), was greater than growth of manufacturing in Oceania (-0.27%).

Comparison with neighbors. The sector of manufacturing in the Solomon Islands was 3.3 times higher than in Vanuatu ($27.6 million) and 3.9 times higher than in Nauru ($23.7 million); but 11.1 times lower than in New Caledonia ($1.0 billion) and 4.9 times lower than in Papua New Guinea ($445.9 million). The value added of manufacturing per capita in the Solomon Islands was 49.4% higher than in Vanuatu ($103.0) and 2.8 times higher than in Papua New Guinea ($55.5); but 24.6 times lower than in New Caledonia ($3.8 thousand) and 14.9 times lower than in Nauru ($2.3 thousand). The growth of manufacturing in the Solomon Islands was greater than in New Caledonia (-0.097%) and in Papua New Guinea (-0.40%); but less than in Nauru (5.7%) and in Vanuatu (4.0%).

Comparison with leaders. The manufacturing of the Solomon Islands was 33 940.2 times lower than in China ($3.1 trillion), 22 559.1 times lower than in the USA ($2.1 trillion), 11 549.1 times lower than in Japan ($1.1 trillion), 8 010.2 times lower than in Germany ($735.2 billion), and 4 254.8 times lower than in South Korea ($390.5 billion). The sector of manufacturing per capita in the Solomon Islands was 58.4 times lower than in Germany ($9.0 thousand), 53.9 times lower than in Japan ($8.3 thousand), 50.2 times lower than in South Korea ($7.7 thousand), 42.1 times lower than in the USA ($6.5 thousand), and 14.4 times lower than in China ($2.2 thousand). The growth of manufacturing in the Solomon Islands was greater than in the USA (1.9%); but less than in China (7.5%), in South Korea (3.8%), in Germany (3.5%), and in Japan (3.0%).

Chapter VI. Construction

(ISIC F)

The value added of construction in the Solomon Islands enlarged from $2.5 million per year in the 1970s to $48.9 million per year in the 2010s, that is by $46.4 million or 19.4 times. The change occurred at $43.4 million due to a 8.9-fold increase in prices, as also at -$2.4 million due to a 1.4-fold decrease in productivity, as well as at $5.4 million due to the rise in population. The average annual growth in construction is 3.1%. The minimum value of construction was in 1970 at $1.2 million. The maximum value of construction was in 2019 at $76.0 million.

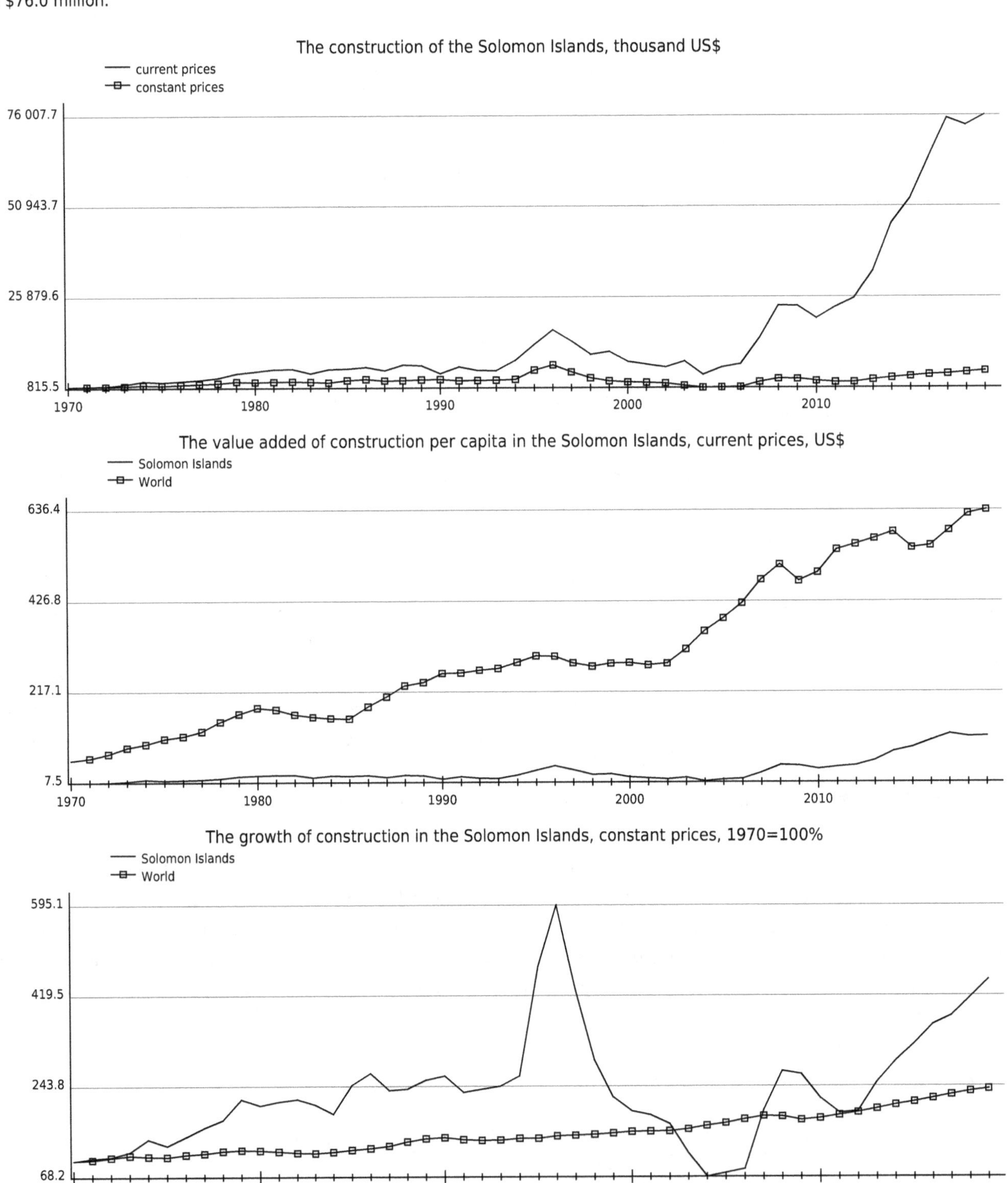

The construction of the Solomon Islands, thousand US$

The value added of construction per capita in the Solomon Islands, current prices, US$

The growth of construction in the Solomon Islands, constant prices, 1970=100%

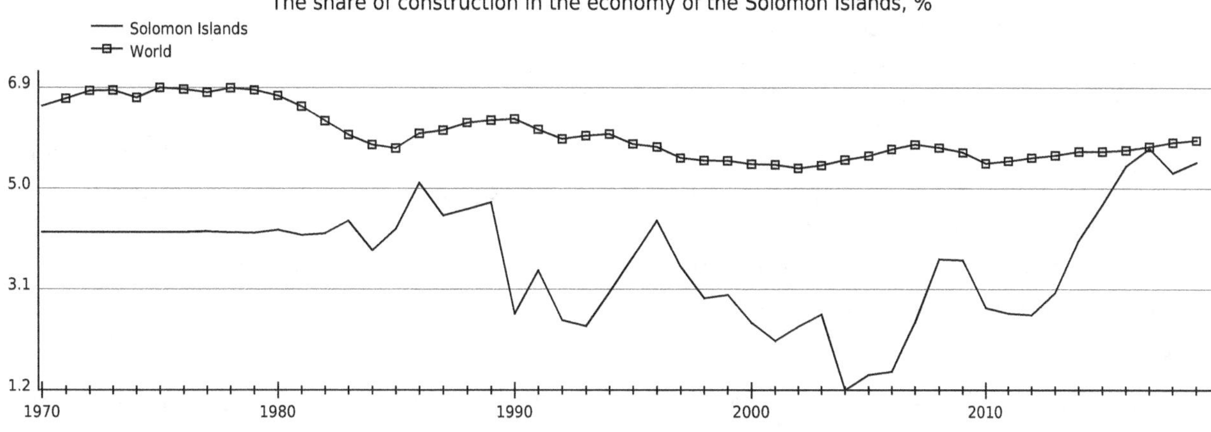

The 1970s

The value of construction in the Solomon Islands was $2.5 million per year in the 1970s, ranked 169th in the world. The share in the world was 0.0006%, and 0.028% in Oceania.

The share of construction in the economy of the Solomon Islands was 4.2% in the 1970s, ranked 136th in the world, and was on a par with Niger (4.1%).

The value of construction per capita in the Solomon Islands was $13.2 in the 1970s, ranked 146th in the world, and was on a par with Mauritania ($13.2), Vanuatu ($13.1). The value of construction per capita in the Solomon Islands was less than construction per capita in the world ($106.1) in 8.0 times, and was less than construction per capita in Oceania ($415.3) in 31.4 times.

The growth of construction in the Solomon Islands was 9.1% in the 1970s, ranked 39th in the world, and was on a par with Hong Kong (9.0%), Aruba (9.1%), Saint Lucia (9.2%). The growth of construction in the Solomon Islands (9.1%) was greater than growth of construction in the world (2.1%), was greater than growth of construction in Oceania (1.7%).

Comparison with neighbors. The value of construction in the Solomon Islands was greater than in Vanuatu ($1.3 million) and in Nauru ($1.1 million); but less than in Papua New Guinea ($91.9 million) and in New Caledonia ($76.5 million). The Solomon Islands construction per capita was greater than in Vanuatu ($13.1); but less than in New Caledonia ($606.3), in Nauru ($161.4), and in Papua New Guinea ($29.5). The growth of construction in the Solomon Islands was greater than in Vanuatu (7.7%), in Papua New Guinea (2.7%), and in Nauru (1.1%); but less than in New Caledonia (13.2%).

Comparison with leaders. The value of construction in the Solomon Islands was less than in the USA ($81.1 billion), in the USSR ($52.5 billion), in Japan ($43.5 billion), in Germany ($33.8 billion), and in France ($22.4 billion). The sector of construction per capita in the Solomon Islands was less than in Germany ($428.6), in France ($417.3), in Japan ($390.8), in the United States ($371.5), and in the USSR ($208.1). The growth of construction in the Solomon Islands was greater than in the USSR (6.5%), in Japan (3.4%), in France (2.0%), in Germany (0.66%), and in the United States (0.31%).

The 1980s

The construction of the Solomon Islands was $6.1 million per year in the 1980s, ranked 168th in the world. The share in the world was 0.0007%, and 0.036% in Oceania.

The share of construction in the economy of the Solomon Islands was 4.4% in the 1980s, ranked 133rd in the world, and was on a par with the USA (4.3%).

The Solomon Islands construction per capita was $22.7 in the 1980s, ranked 144th in the world, and was on a par with Haiti ($22.9), Mauritania ($22.2). The sector of construction per capita in the Solomon Islands was less than construction per capita in the world ($186.2) in 8.2 times, and was less than construction per capita in Oceania ($677.4) in 29.8 times.

The growth of construction in the Solomon Islands was 1.6% in the 1980s, ranked 108th in the world. The growth of construction in the Solomon Islands (1.6%) was less than growth of construction in the world (1.7%), was less than growth of construction in Oceania (2.8%).

Comparison with neighbors. The value added of construction in the Solomon Islands was greater than in Vanuatu ($2.4 million) and in

Nauru ($1.6 million); but less than in Papua New Guinea ($133.8 million) and in New Caledonia ($63.6 million). The value added of construction per capita in the Solomon Islands was greater than in Vanuatu ($18.8); but less than in New Caledonia ($409.4), in Nauru ($183.8), and in Papua New Guinea ($33.2). The growth of construction in the Solomon Islands was greater than in Nauru (-2.4%) and in New Caledonia (-3.6%); but less than in Vanuatu (7.3%) and in Papua New Guinea (5.3%).

Comparison with leaders. The sector of construction in the Solomon Islands was less than in the USA ($180.6 billion), in Japan ($138.7 billion), in the USSR ($72.1 billion), in Germany ($57.8 billion), and in France ($42.5 billion). The sector of construction per capita in the Solomon Islands was less than in Japan ($1 143.9), in the USA ($754.4), in France ($751.9), in Germany ($740.2), and in the USSR ($262.0). The growth of construction in the Solomon Islands was greater than in the United States (1.1%), in France (0.67%), and in Germany (-0.52%); but less than in the USSR (6.2%) and in Japan (2.1%).

The 1990s

The value added of construction in the Solomon Islands was $9.5 million per year in the 1990s, ranked 195th in the world. The share in the world was 0.0006%, and 0.037% in Oceania.

The share of construction in the economy of the Solomon Islands was 3.2% in the 1990s, ranked 177th in the world, and was on a par with Madagascar (3.2%), Zambia (3.3%).

The value added of construction per capita in the Solomon Islands was $26.7 in the 1990s, ranked 162nd in the world. The construction per capita in the Solomon Islands was less than construction per capita in the world ($278.6) in 10.4 times, and was less than construction per capita in Oceania ($881.0) in 33.0 times.

The growth of construction in the Solomon Islands was -1.4% in the 1990s, ranked 159th in the world. The growth of construction in the Solomon Islands (-1.4%) was less than growth of construction in the world (0.71%), was less than growth of construction in Oceania (3.0%).

Comparison with neighbors. The construction of the Solomon Islands was greater than in Vanuatu ($5.8 million) and in Nauru ($1.4 million); but less than in Papua New Guinea ($212.9 million) and in New Caledonia ($208.0 million). The value of construction per capita in the Solomon Islands was less than in New Caledonia ($1 088.4), in Nauru ($139.4), in Papua New Guinea ($41.4), and in Vanuatu ($35.0). The growth of construction in the Solomon Islands was greater than in Nauru (-13.6%); but less than in New Caledonia (8.7%), in Papua New Guinea (2.0%), and in Vanuatu (-0.34%).

Comparison with leaders. The Solomon Islands construction was less than in Japan ($343.2 billion), in the USA ($299.1 billion), in Germany ($125.2 billion), in the UK ($69.8 billion), and in France ($68.8 billion). The value of construction per capita in the Solomon Islands was less than in Japan ($2.7 thousand), in Germany ($1 552.3), in the United Kingdom ($1 205.1), in France ($1 158.8), and in the USA ($1 131.2). The growth of construction in the Solomon Islands was less than in the United States (1.8%), in Germany (-0.047%), in the United Kingdom (-0.34%), in France (-0.65%), and in Japan (-1.0%).

The 2000s

The value of construction in the Solomon Islands was $10.9 million per year in the 2000s, ranked 201st in the world. The share in the world was 0.0004%, and 0.020% in Oceania.

The share of construction in the economy of the Solomon Islands was 2.5% in the 2000s, ranked 199th in the world, and was on a par with Puerto Rico (2.5%).

The construction per capita in the Solomon Islands was $23.5 in the 2000s, ranked 186th in the world, and was on a par with Senegal ($23.3), Kenya ($23.8), Madagascar ($24.0). The sector of construction per capita in the Solomon Islands was less than construction per capita in the world ($381.3) in 16.2 times, and was less than construction per capita in Oceania ($1 644.6) in 70.0 times.

The growth of construction in the Solomon Islands was 1.8% in the 2000s, ranked 150th in the world, and was on a par with Paraguay (1.8%), Thailand (1.8%). The growth of construction in the Solomon Islands (1.8%) was greater than growth of construction in the world (1.5%), was less than growth of construction in Oceania (4.8%).

Comparison with neighbors. The sector of construction in the Solomon Islands was greater than in Nauru ($1.2 million); but less than in New Caledonia ($558.1 million), in Papua New Guinea ($414.8 million), and in Vanuatu ($14.1 million). The Solomon Islands construction per capita was less than in New Caledonia ($2.4 thousand), in Nauru ($121.4), in Vanuatu ($68.3), and in Papua New Guinea ($64.3). The growth of construction in the Solomon Islands was greater than in Nauru (-1.3%); but less than in Papua New

Guinea (14.2%), in Vanuatu (12.2%), and in New Caledonia (5.4%).

Comparison with leaders. The sector of construction in the Solomon Islands was less than in the USA ($583.0 billion), in Japan ($270.5 billion), in China ($150.1 billion), in the UK ($132.1 billion), and in Spain ($111.8 billion). The value added of construction per capita in the Solomon Islands was less than in Spain ($2.6 thousand), in the UK ($2.2 thousand), in Japan ($2.1 thousand), in the USA ($1 983.7), and in China ($113.1). The growth of construction in the Solomon Islands was greater than in Spain (1.7%), in the UK (0.17%), in the United States (-2.6%), and in Japan (-3.9%); but less than in China (11.9%).

The 2010s

The construction of the Solomon Islands was $48.9 million per year in the 2010s, ranked 190th in the world. The share in the world was 0.0012%, and 0.039% in Oceania.

The share of construction in the economy of the Solomon Islands was 4.4% in the 2010s, ranked 160th in the world, and was on a par with Burkina Faso (4.3%), Hungary (4.3%).

The sector of construction per capita in the Solomon Islands was $82.0 in the 2010s, ranked 172nd in the world, and was on a par with Bolivia ($84.1). The construction per capita in the Solomon Islands was less than construction per capita in the world ($572.1) in 7.0 times, and was less than construction per capita in Oceania ($3 171.9) in 38.7 times.

The growth of construction in the Solomon Islands was 5.4% in the 2010s, ranked 63rd in the world. The growth of construction in the Solomon Islands (5.4%) was greater than growth of construction in the world (2.9%), was greater than growth of construction in Oceania (1.7%).

Comparison with neighbors. The Solomon Islands construction was 35.5% higher than in Vanuatu ($36.1 million) and 14.6 times higher than in Nauru ($3.4 million); but 35.5 times lower than in Papua New Guinea ($1.7 billion) and 22.5 times lower than in New Caledonia ($1.1 billion). The value added of construction per capita in the Solomon Islands was 50.0 times lower than in New Caledonia ($4.1 thousand), 4.0 times lower than in Nauru ($324.1), 2.6 times lower than in Papua New Guinea ($216.4), and 39.2% lower than in Vanuatu ($134.9). The growth of construction in the Solomon Islands was greater than in New Caledonia (3.8%), in Papua New Guinea (2.6%), and in Vanuatu (1.8%); but less than in Nauru (8.2%).

Comparison with leaders. The construction of the Solomon Islands was 14 944.7 times lower than in China ($731.1 billion), 13 916.6 times lower than in the United States ($680.8 billion), 5 696.3 times lower than in Japan ($278.7 billion), 3 436.1 times lower than in India ($168.1 billion), and 3 132.2 times lower than in Germany ($153.2 billion). The construction per capita in the Solomon Islands was 26.6 times lower than in Japan ($2.2 thousand), 26.0 times lower than in the USA ($2.1 thousand), 22.8 times lower than in Germany ($1 871.9), 6.4 times lower than in China ($521.3), and 36.5% lower than in India ($129.1). The growth of construction in the Solomon Islands was greater than in India (5.2%), in Germany (1.8%), in Japan (1.7%), and in the USA (1.4%); but less than in China (8.2%).

Chapter VII. Transportation

Transport, storage and communication (ISIC I)

The value of transportation in the Solomon Islands rose from $3.2 million per year in the 1970s to $63.1 million per year in the 2010s, that is by $59.9 million or 19.8 times. The change occurred at $39.2 million due to a 2.6-fold increase in prices, as also at $14.0 million due to a 2.4-fold increase in productivity, as well as at $6.8 million due to the growth in population. The average annual growth in transportation is 5.3%. The minimum value of transportation was in 1970 at $1.5 million. The maximum value of transportation was in 2018 at $74.3 million.

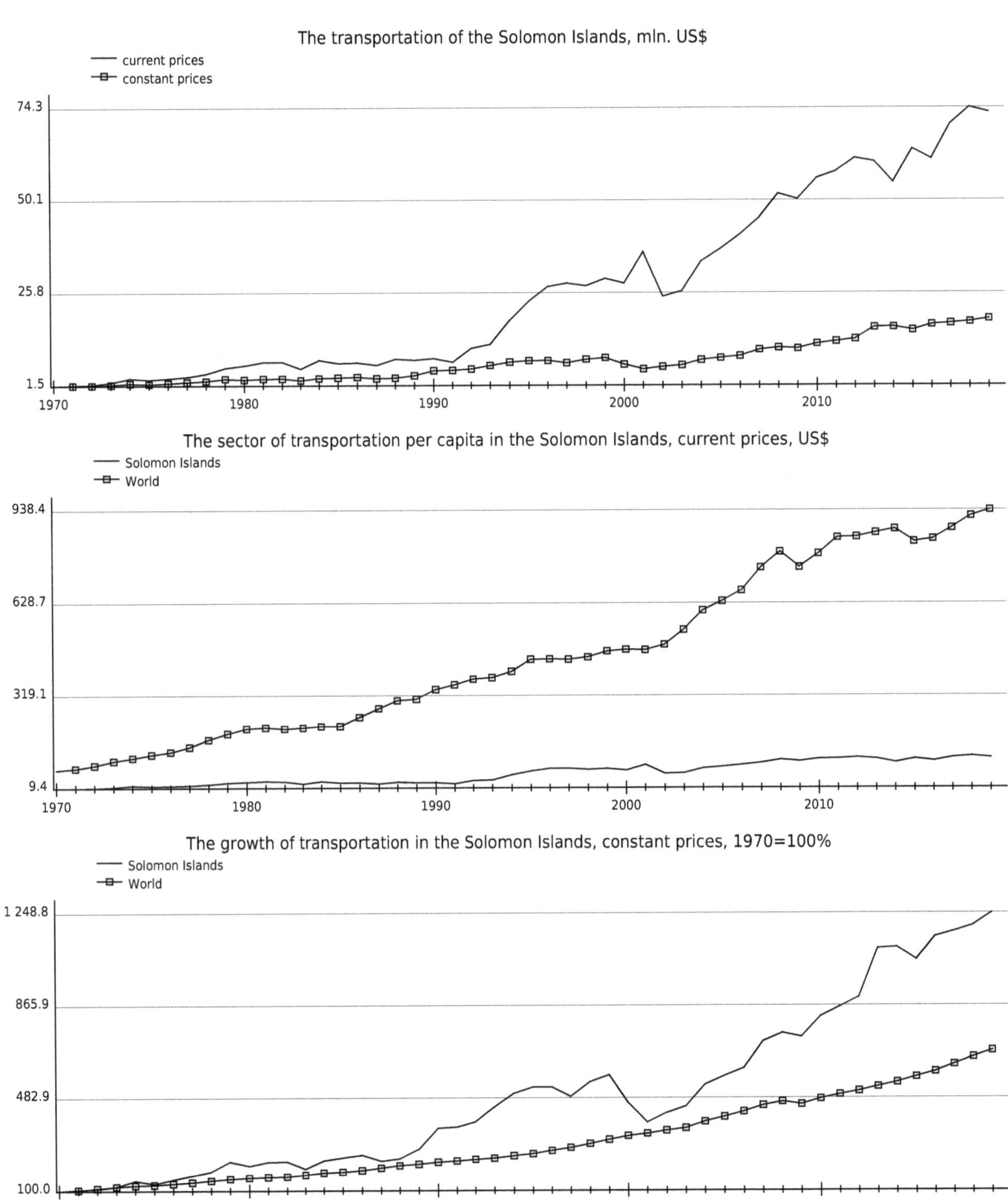

The transportation of the Solomon Islands, mln. US$

The sector of transportation per capita in the Solomon Islands, current prices, US$

The growth of transportation in the Solomon Islands, constant prices, 1970=100%

The 1970s

The Solomon Islands transportation was $3.2 million per year in the 1970s, ranked 169th in the world. The share in the world was 0.0006%, and 0.035% in Oceania.

The share of transportation in the economy of the Solomon Islands was 5.3% in the 1970s, ranked 124th in the world, and was on a par with Kenya (5.2%).

The value added of transportation per capita in the Solomon Islands was $16.7 in the 1970s, ranked 149th in the world, and was on a par with Pakistan ($16.5), El Salvador ($16.5). The Solomon Islands transportation per capita was less than transportation per capita in the world ($122.3) in 7.3 times, and was less than transportation per capita in Oceania ($423.7) in 25.3 times.

The growth of transportation in the Solomon Islands was 9.1% in the 1970s, ranked 30th in the world, and was on a par with the Seychelles (9.1%), Aruba (9.1%), South-Eastern Asia (9.2%). The growth of transportation in the Solomon Islands (9.1%) was greater than growth of transportation in the world (4.6%), was greater than growth of transportation in Oceania (4.9%).

Comparison with neighbors. The Solomon Islands transportation was less than in Papua New Guinea ($305.2 million), in New Caledonia ($25.2 million), in Vanuatu ($7.5 million), and in Nauru ($5.7 million). The sector of transportation per capita in the Solomon Islands was less than in Nauru ($795.9), in New Caledonia ($200.0), in Papua New Guinea ($98.1), and in Vanuatu ($76.3). The growth of transportation in the Solomon Islands was greater than in Vanuatu (7.7%), in Papua New Guinea (3.1%), in New Caledonia (2.9%), and in Nauru (1.1%).

Comparison with leaders. The transportation of the Solomon Islands was less than in the United States ($168.6 billion), in Japan ($46.4 billion), in Germany ($29.6 billion), in the USSR ($28.8 billion), and in France ($24.0 billion). The transportation per capita in the Solomon Islands was less than in the USA ($772.4), in France ($447.4), in Japan ($416.6), in Germany ($376.1), and in the USSR ($114.0). The growth of transportation in the Solomon Islands was greater than in the USSR (8.1%), in the USA (4.2%), in France (4.1%), in Germany (3.0%), and in Japan (1.7%).

The 1980s

The sector of transportation in the Solomon Islands was $7.4 million per year in the 1980s, ranked 172nd in the world. The share in the world was 0.0006%, and 0.034% in Oceania.

The share of transportation in the economy of the Solomon Islands was 5.4% in the 1980s, ranked 134th in the world, and was on a par with Poland (5.4%), the Virgin Islands (5.4%).

The value added of transportation per capita in the Solomon Islands was $27.9 in the 1980s, ranked 152nd in the world. The sector of transportation per capita in the Solomon Islands was less than transportation per capita in the world ($242.0) in 8.7 times, and was less than transportation per capita in Oceania ($872.5) in 31.3 times.

The growth of transportation in the Solomon Islands was 2.1% in the 1980s, ranked 140th in the world, and was on a par with Middle Africa (2.1%), Belgium (2.1%). The growth of transportation in the Solomon Islands (2.1%) was less than growth of transportation in the world (3.4%), was less than growth of transportation in Oceania (4.2%).

Comparison with neighbors. The Solomon Islands transportation was less than in Papua New Guinea ($389.0 million), in New

Caledonia ($52.2 million), in Vanuatu ($12.6 million), and in Nauru ($7.7 million). The sector of transportation per capita in the Solomon Islands was less than in Nauru ($906.3), in New Caledonia ($336.4), in Vanuatu ($97.7), and in Papua New Guinea ($96.5). The growth of transportation in the Solomon Islands was greater than in Papua New Guinea (0.77%) and in Nauru (-2.4%); but less than in New Caledonia (7.4%) and in Vanuatu (2.4%).

Comparison with leaders. The transportation of the Solomon Islands was less than in the USA ($394.9 billion), in Japan ($147.7 billion), in Germany ($56.6 billion), in France ($56.2 billion), and in the United Kingdom ($53.0 billion). The value of transportation per capita in the Solomon Islands was less than in the USA ($1 649.2), in Japan ($1 217.8), in France ($993.7), in the United Kingdom ($938.7), and in Germany ($725.5). The growth of transportation in the Solomon Islands was greater than in Germany (1.8%); but less than in France (5.4%), in Japan (4.7%), in the USA (3.6%), and in the UK (3.0%).

The 1990s

The transportation of the Solomon Islands was $19.4 million per year in the 1990s, ranked 196th in the world. The share in the world was 0.0008%, and 0.050% in Oceania.

The share of transportation in the economy of the Solomon Islands was 6.7% in the 1990s, ranked 141st in the world, and was on a par with the Cayman Islands (6.6%), Paraguay (6.6%).

The Solomon Islands transportation per capita was $54.7 in the 1990s, ranked 148th in the world, and was on a par with Pakistan ($54.7), the Philippines ($53.9), Azerbaijan ($55.5). The Solomon Islands transportation per capita was less than transportation per capita in the world ($409.5) in 7.5 times, and was less than transportation per capita in Oceania ($1 336.3) in 24.4 times.

The growth of transportation in the Solomon Islands was 7.8% in the 1990s, ranked 34th in the world, and was on a par with Belize (7.8%). The growth of transportation in the Solomon Islands (7.8%) was greater than growth of transportation in the world (4.0%), was greater than growth of transportation in Oceania (4.7%).

Comparison with neighbors. The transportation of the Solomon Islands was greater than in Nauru ($7.1 million); but less than in Papua New Guinea ($613.2 million), in New Caledonia ($202.2 million), and in Vanuatu ($22.2 million). The value of transportation per capita in the Solomon Islands was less than in New Caledonia ($1 058.4), in Nauru ($687.3), in Vanuatu ($134.6), and in Papua New Guinea ($119.2). The growth of transportation in the Solomon Islands was greater than in New Caledonia (7.1%), in Papua New Guinea (2.4%), in Vanuatu (1.3%), and in Nauru (-12.9%).

Comparison with leaders. The Solomon Islands transportation was less than in the United States ($702.6 billion), in Japan ($373.9 billion), in Germany ($144.3 billion), in France ($118.7 billion), and in the United Kingdom ($117.6 billion). The value added of transportation per capita in the Solomon Islands was less than in Japan ($3.0 thousand), in the USA ($2.7 thousand), in the United Kingdom ($2.0 thousand), in France ($1 999.2), and in Germany ($1 789.0). The growth of transportation in the Solomon Islands was greater than in the United States (5.0%), in France (4.8%), in the UK (4.7%), in Germany (3.9%), and in Japan (3.0%).

The 2000s

The Solomon Islands transportation was $37.5 million per year in the 2000s, ranked 195th in the world. The share in the world was 0.0009%, and 0.056% in Oceania.

The share of transportation in the economy of the Solomon Islands was 8.6% in the 2000s, ranked 115th in the world, and was on a par with Central America (8.6%), Mexico (8.6%), Spain (8.6%).

The Solomon Islands transportation per capita was $80.9 in the 2000s, ranked 161st in the world, and was on a par with Cameroon ($79.2). The sector of transportation per capita in the Solomon Islands was less than transportation per capita in the world ($621.1) in 7.7 times, and was less than transportation per capita in Oceania ($2 009.1) in 24.8 times.

The growth of transportation in the Solomon Islands was 2.5% in the 2000s, ranked 159th in the world, and was on a par with Monaco (2.4%), Saint Lucia (2.5%), Canada (2.5%). The growth of transportation in the Solomon Islands (2.5%) was less than growth of transportation in the world (3.9%), was less than growth of transportation in Oceania (3.7%).

Comparison with neighbors. The value added of transportation in the Solomon Islands was greater than in Nauru ($4.7 million); but less than in New Caledonia ($410.4 million), in Papua New Guinea ($292.6 million), and in Vanuatu ($38.7 million). The sector of transportation per capita in the Solomon Islands was greater than in Papua New Guinea ($45.3); but less than in New Caledonia ($1 751.6), in Nauru ($468.2), and in Vanuatu ($187.2). The growth of transportation in the Solomon Islands was greater than in Papua

New Guinea (0.29%) and in Nauru (-8.2%); but less than in Vanuatu (4.6%) and in New Caledonia (3.0%).

Comparison with leaders. The sector of transportation in the Solomon Islands was less than in the USA ($1.2 trillion), in Japan ($468.5 billion), in Germany ($228.2 billion), in the UK ($215.9 billion), and in France ($185.6 billion). The Solomon Islands transportation per capita was less than in the United States ($4.0 thousand), in Japan ($3.7 thousand), in the UK ($3.6 thousand), in France ($3.0 thousand), and in Germany ($2.8 thousand). The growth of transportation in the Solomon Islands was greater than in Japan (1.5%); but less than in Germany (3.4%), in the United Kingdom (3.1%), in the USA (3.1%), and in France (2.7%).

The 2010s

The value of transportation in the Solomon Islands was $63.1 million per year in the 2010s, ranked 196th in the world. The share in the world was 0.0010%, and 0.052% in Oceania.

The share of transportation in the economy of the Solomon Islands was 5.6% in the 2010s, ranked 178th in the world, and was on a par with Nicaragua (5.6%), Andorra (5.6%), Venezuela (5.7%).

The value of transportation per capita in the Solomon Islands was $105.8 in the 2010s, ranked 174th in the world, and was on a par with Papua New Guinea ($108.5). The sector of transportation per capita in the Solomon Islands was less than transportation per capita in the world ($864.8) in 8.2 times, and was less than transportation per capita in Oceania ($3 066.3) in 29.0 times.

The growth of transportation in the Solomon Islands was 5.4% in the 2010s, ranked 73rd in the world, and was on a par with the Philippines (5.4%), Belarus (5.4%), Southern Asia (5.5%). The growth of transportation in the Solomon Islands (5.4%) was greater than growth of transportation in the world (4.0%), was greater than growth of transportation in Oceania (2.3%).

Comparison with neighbors. The transportation of the Solomon Islands was 2.9 times higher than in Nauru ($22.0 million); but 13.8 times lower than in Papua New Guinea ($871.9 million), 10.2 times lower than in New Caledonia ($646.9 million), and 14.9% lower than in Vanuatu ($74.2 million). The sector of transportation per capita in the Solomon Islands was 22.7 times lower than in New Caledonia ($2.4 thousand), 20.0 times lower than in Nauru ($2.1 thousand), 2.6 times lower than in Vanuatu ($277.2), and 2.5% lower than in Papua New Guinea ($108.5). The growth of transportation in the Solomon Islands was greater than in Papua New Guinea (4.8%), in Vanuatu (3.8%), and in New Caledonia (2.8%); but less than in Nauru (17.4%).

Comparison with leaders. The value of transportation in the Solomon Islands was 28 330.9 times lower than in the USA ($1.8 trillion), 8 393.2 times lower than in Japan ($529.8 billion), 7 354.2 times lower than in China ($464.2 billion), 4 752.8 times lower than in Germany ($300.0 billion), and 4 083.0 times lower than in the United Kingdom ($257.7 billion). The sector of transportation per capita in the Solomon Islands was 52.9 times lower than in the United States ($5.6 thousand), 39.1 times lower than in Japan ($4.1 thousand), 37.1 times lower than in the UK ($3.9 thousand), 34.6 times lower than in Germany ($3.7 thousand), and 3.1 times lower than in China ($331.0). The growth of transportation in the Solomon Islands was greater than in the USA (5.1%), in the UK (2.8%), in Germany (2.7%), and in Japan (0.81%); but less than in China (7.5%).

Chapter VIII. Trade

Wholesale, retail trade, restaurants and hotels (ISIC G-H)

The Solomon Islands trade rose from $6.2 million per year in the 1970s to $237.4 million per year in the 2010s, that is by $231.2 million or 38.6 times. The change occurred at $200.7 million due to a 6.5-fold increase in prices, as also at $17.4 million due to a 1.9-fold increase in productivity, as well as at $13.1 million due to the increase in population. The average annual growth in trade is 4.9%. The minimum value of trade was in 1970 at $2.9 million. The maximum value of trade was in 2018 at $306.7 million.

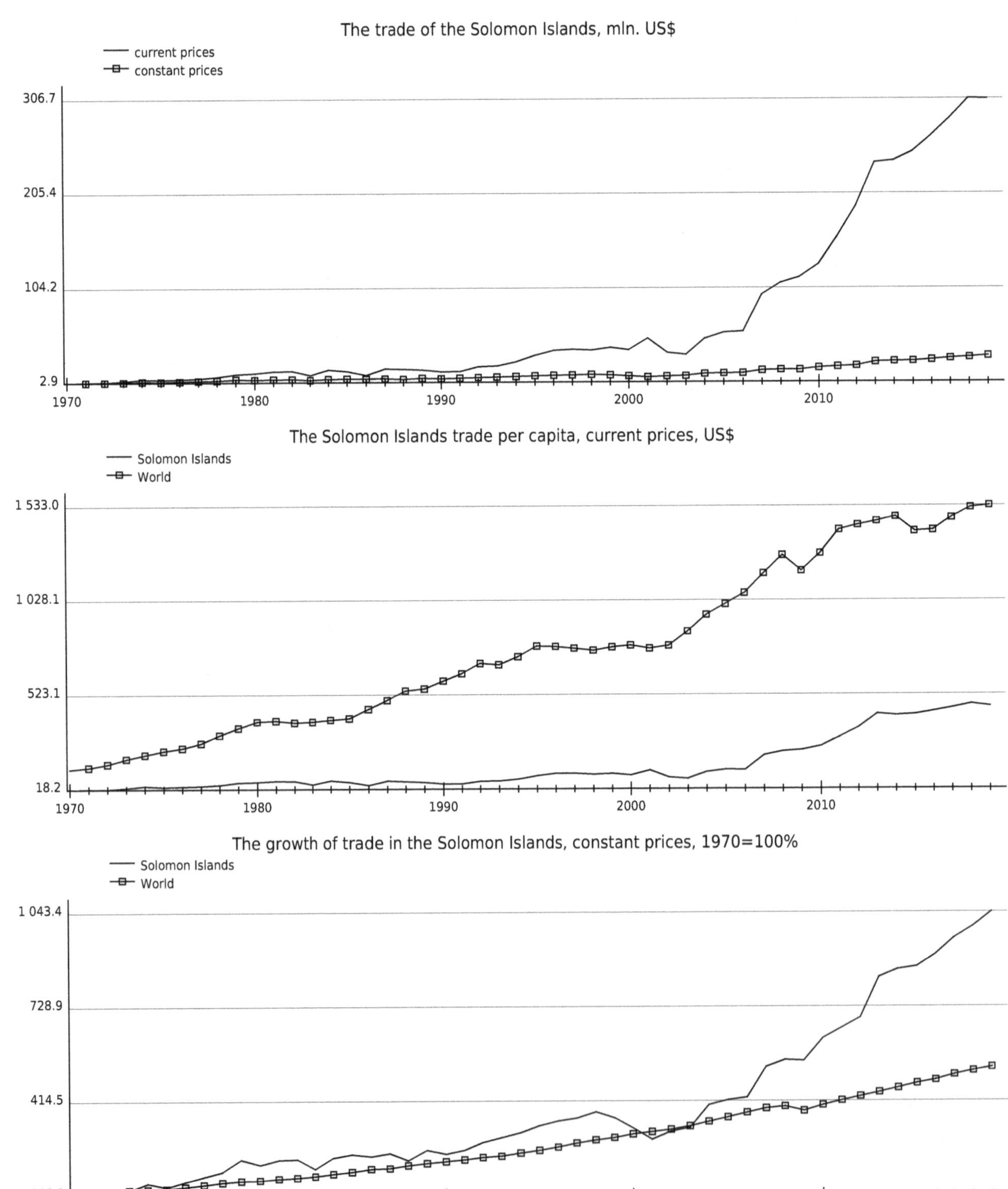

The trade of the Solomon Islands, mln. US$

The Solomon Islands trade per capita, current prices, US$

The growth of trade in the Solomon Islands, constant prices, 1970=100%

The 1970s

The value added of trade in the Solomon Islands was $6.2 million per year in the 1970s, ranked 170th in the world. The share in the world was 0.0007%, and 0.048% in Oceania.

The share of trade in the economy of the Solomon Islands was 10.2% in the 1970s, ranked 148th in the world, and was on a par with Iceland (10.3%).

The value added of trade per capita in the Solomon Islands was $32.3 in the 1970s, ranked 157th in the world, and was on a par with Niger ($32.2), Equatorial Guinea ($32.4), Uganda ($32.0). The value added of trade per capita in the Solomon Islands was less than trade per capita in the world ($221.0) in 6.8 times, and was less than trade per capita in Oceania ($597.4) in 18.5 times.

The growth of trade in the Solomon Islands was 9.2% in the 1970s, ranked 22nd in the world, and was on a par with Aruba (9.1%), Iran (9.2%). The growth of trade in the Solomon Islands (9.2%) was greater than growth of trade in the world (4.5%), was greater than growth of trade in Oceania (1.6%).

Comparison with neighbors. The value added of trade in the Solomon Islands was greater than in Nauru ($5.1 million); but less than in Papua New Guinea ($634.4 million), in New Caledonia ($148.5 million), and in Vanuatu ($12.6 million). The Solomon Islands trade per capita was less than in New Caledonia ($1 177.7), in Nauru ($715.9), in Papua New Guinea ($203.8), and in Vanuatu ($128.0). The growth of trade in the Solomon Islands was greater than in Vanuatu (7.7%), in Papua New Guinea (3.1%), in Nauru (1.1%), and in New Caledonia (-3.8%).

Comparison with leaders. The Solomon Islands trade was less than in the USA ($278.3 billion), in Japan ($90.3 billion), in the USSR ($62.3 billion), in Germany ($61.1 billion), and in France ($40.9 billion). The sector of trade per capita in the Solomon Islands was less than in the United States ($1 275.1), in Japan ($811.1), in Germany ($775.5), in France ($762.4), and in the USSR ($247.1). The growth of trade in the Solomon Islands was greater than in Japan (8.2%), in the USSR (5.2%), in France (3.9%), in the USA (3.9%), and in Germany (3.0%).

The 1980s

The value added of trade in the Solomon Islands was $14.7 million per year in the 1980s, ranked 171st in the world. The share in the world was 0.0007%, and 0.050% in Oceania.

The share of trade in the economy of the Solomon Islands was 10.6% in the 1980s, ranked 153rd in the world, and was on a par with Ethiopia (10.6%), Burundi (10.6%), Macao (10.6%).

The trade per capita in the Solomon Islands was $55.1 in the 1980s, ranked 155th in the world, and was on a par with DR Congo ($54.8), Mozambique ($54.7). The value of trade per capita in the Solomon Islands was less than trade per capita in the world ($437.7) in 7.9 times, and was less than trade per capita in Oceania ($1 193.9) in 21.7 times.

The growth of trade in the Solomon Islands was 1.3% in the 1980s, ranked 137th in the world, and was on a par with Bhutan (1.3%). The growth of trade in the Solomon Islands (1.3%) was less than growth of trade in the world (3.3%), was less than growth of trade in Oceania (2.5%).

Comparison with neighbors. The trade of the Solomon Islands was greater than in Nauru ($6.9 million); but less than in Papua New

Guinea ($971.9 million), in New Caledonia ($298.4 million), and in Vanuatu ($23.8 million). The Solomon Islands trade per capita was less than in New Caledonia ($1 921.1), in Nauru ($815.4), in Papua New Guinea ($241.1), and in Vanuatu ($184.8). The growth of trade in the Solomon Islands was greater than in Nauru (-2.4%); but less than in New Caledonia (4.9%), in Vanuatu (3.6%), and in Papua New Guinea (1.5%).

Comparison with leaders. The sector of trade in the Solomon Islands was less than in the United States ($653.3 billion), in Japan ($277.3 billion), in Germany ($116.7 billion), in the USSR ($112.3 billion), and in Italy ($95.7 billion). The sector of trade per capita in the Solomon Islands was less than in the USA ($2.7 thousand), in Japan ($2.3 thousand), in Italy ($1 684.2), in Germany ($1 496.0), and in the USSR ($408.1). The growth of trade in the Solomon Islands was greater than in the USSR (-0.62%); but less than in Japan (4.9%), in the USA (4.4%), in Italy (2.3%), and in Germany (1.8%).

The 1990s

The value added of trade in the Solomon Islands was $27.7 million per year in the 1990s, ranked 196th in the world. The share in the world was 0.0007%, and 0.050% in Oceania.

The share of trade in the economy of the Solomon Islands was 9.5% in the 1990s, ranked 179th in the world, and was on a par with Belarus (9.5%), Malawi (9.6%).

The value of trade per capita in the Solomon Islands was $78.0 in the 1990s, ranked 163rd in the world. The trade per capita in the Solomon Islands was less than trade per capita in the world ($721.8) in 9.3 times, and was less than trade per capita in Oceania ($1 916.7) in 24.6 times.

The growth of trade in the Solomon Islands was 3.6% in the 1990s, ranked 89th in the world, and was on a par with Cambodia (3.6%), Iceland (3.6%). The growth of trade in the Solomon Islands (3.6%) was greater than growth of trade in the world (3.5%), was greater than growth of trade in Oceania (3.3%).

Comparison with neighbors. The value added of trade in the Solomon Islands was greater than in Nauru ($6.4 million); but less than in Papua New Guinea ($1.3 billion), in New Caledonia ($608.0 million), and in Vanuatu ($45.7 million). The value added of trade per capita in the Solomon Islands was less than in New Caledonia ($3.2 thousand), in Nauru ($618.9), in Vanuatu ($276.9), and in Papua New Guinea ($249.8). The growth of trade in the Solomon Islands was greater than in Papua New Guinea (-2.1%), in New Caledonia (-4.2%), and in Nauru (-13.2%); but less than in Vanuatu (4.3%).

Comparison with leaders. The Solomon Islands trade was less than in the United States ($1.2 trillion), in Japan ($713.2 billion), in Germany ($243.7 billion), in Italy ($185.6 billion), and in France ($177.0 billion). The value added of trade per capita in the Solomon Islands was less than in Japan ($5.7 thousand), in the USA ($4.4 thousand), in Italy ($3.3 thousand), in Germany ($3.0 thousand), and in France ($3.0 thousand). The growth of trade in the Solomon Islands was greater than in Germany (2.5%), in France (2.4%), and in Italy (1.9%); but less than in the USA (4.3%) and in Japan (3.8%).

The 2000s

The value added of trade in the Solomon Islands was $63.7 million per year in the 2000s, ranked 195th in the world. The share in the world was 0.0010%, and 0.065% in Oceania.

The share of trade in the economy of the Solomon Islands was 14.6% in the 2000s, ranked 109th in the world, and was on a par with Europe (14.6%), Belgium (14.7%), Moldova (14.6%).

The value added of trade per capita in the Solomon Islands was $137.3 in the 2000s, ranked 165th in the world, and was on a par with Mauritania ($137.7), Sudan ($138.3), Iraq ($139.2). The value of trade per capita in the Solomon Islands was less than trade per capita in the world ($990.3) in 7.2 times, and was less than trade per capita in Oceania ($2 922.7) in 21.3 times.

The growth of trade in the Solomon Islands was 4.4% in the 2000s, ranked 91st in the world, and was on a par with Tunisia (4.3%), Togo (4.4%), Kenya (4.4%). The growth of trade in the Solomon Islands (4.4%) was greater than growth of trade in the world (2.7%), was greater than growth of trade in Oceania (3.0%).

Comparison with neighbors. The value of trade in the Solomon Islands was greater than in Nauru ($5.3 million); but less than in Papua New Guinea ($1.0 billion), in New Caledonia ($705.6 million), and in Vanuatu ($79.3 million). The sector of trade per capita in the Solomon Islands was less than in New Caledonia ($3.0 thousand), in Nauru ($532.3), in Vanuatu ($383.3), and in Papua New Guinea ($154.9). The growth of trade in the Solomon Islands was greater than in New Caledonia (4.0%), in Vanuatu (3.6%), and in Nauru

(-2.8%); but less than in Papua New Guinea (4.9%).

Comparison with leaders. The value of trade in the Solomon Islands was less than in the USA ($1.9 trillion), in Japan ($771.8 billion), in Germany ($296.0 billion), in the United Kingdom ($293.5 billion), and in China ($262.0 billion). The sector of trade per capita in the Solomon Islands was less than in the United States ($6.4 thousand), in Japan ($6.0 thousand), in the United Kingdom ($4.9 thousand), in Germany ($3.6 thousand), and in China ($197.5). The growth of trade in the Solomon Islands was greater than in Germany (1.7%), in the UK (1.3%), in the United States (1.1%), and in Japan (-0.77%); but less than in China (11.9%).

The 2010s

The Solomon Islands trade was $237.4 million per year in the 2010s, ranked 185th in the world, and was on a par with Eritrea ($232.7 million). The share in the world was 0.0023%, and 0.13% in Oceania.

The share of trade in the economy of the Solomon Islands was 21.2% in the 2010s, ranked 35th in the world, and was on a par with Cameroon (21.0%), Mexico (21.0%), Kyrgyzstan (21.0%).

The value added of trade per capita in the Solomon Islands was $397.9 in the 2010s, ranked 146th in the world, and was on a par with Jordan ($394.6). The value added of trade per capita in the Solomon Islands was less than trade per capita in the world ($1 436.8) in 3.6 times, and was less than trade per capita in Oceania ($4 550.6) in 11.4 times.

The growth of trade in the Solomon Islands was 6.6% in the 2010s, ranked 28th in the world, and was on a par with Mali (6.6%), the Maldives (6.7%). The growth of trade in the Solomon Islands (6.6%) was greater than growth of trade in the world (3.3%), was greater than growth of trade in Oceania (2.0%).

Comparison with neighbors. The Solomon Islands trade was 32.0% higher than in Vanuatu ($179.9 million) and 10.7 times higher than in Nauru ($22.2 million); but 10.8 times lower than in Papua New Guinea ($2.6 billion) and 4.6 times lower than in New Caledonia ($1.1 billion). The trade per capita in the Solomon Islands was 24.2% higher than in Papua New Guinea ($320.4); but 10.1 times lower than in New Caledonia ($4.0 thousand), 5.4 times lower than in Nauru ($2.1 thousand), and 40.8% lower than in Vanuatu ($672.1). The growth of trade in the Solomon Islands was greater than in Vanuatu (3.2%), in Papua New Guinea (1.7%), and in New Caledonia (0.88%); but less than in Nauru (16.9%).

Comparison with leaders. The value of trade in the Solomon Islands was 11 018.2 times lower than in the United States ($2.6 trillion), 5 031.6 times lower than in China ($1.2 trillion), 3 663.1 times lower than in Japan ($869.5 billion), 1 569.7 times lower than in Germany ($372.6 billion), and 1 390.1 times lower than in the UK ($330.0 billion). The Solomon Islands trade per capita was 20.6 times lower than in the United States ($8.2 thousand), 17.1 times lower than in Japan ($6.8 thousand), 12.6 times lower than in the United Kingdom ($5.0 thousand), 11.4 times lower than in Germany ($4.6 thousand), and 2.1 times lower than in China ($851.7). The growth of trade in the Solomon Islands was greater than in the UK (2.8%), in the United States (2.3%), in Germany (2.0%), and in Japan (0.77%); but less than in China (8.9%).

Chapter IX. Services

(ISIC J-P)

The value added of services in the Solomon Islands grew up from $14.8 million per year in the 1970s to $349.2 million per year in the 2010s, that is by $334.4 million or 23.5 times. The change occurred at $268.8 million due to a 4.3-fold increase in prices, as also at $34.0 million due to a 1.7-fold increase in productivity, as well as at $31.6 million due to the expansion in population. The average annual growth in services is 4.8%. The minimum value of services was in 1970 at $7.0 million. The maximum value of services was in 2018 at $433.4 million.

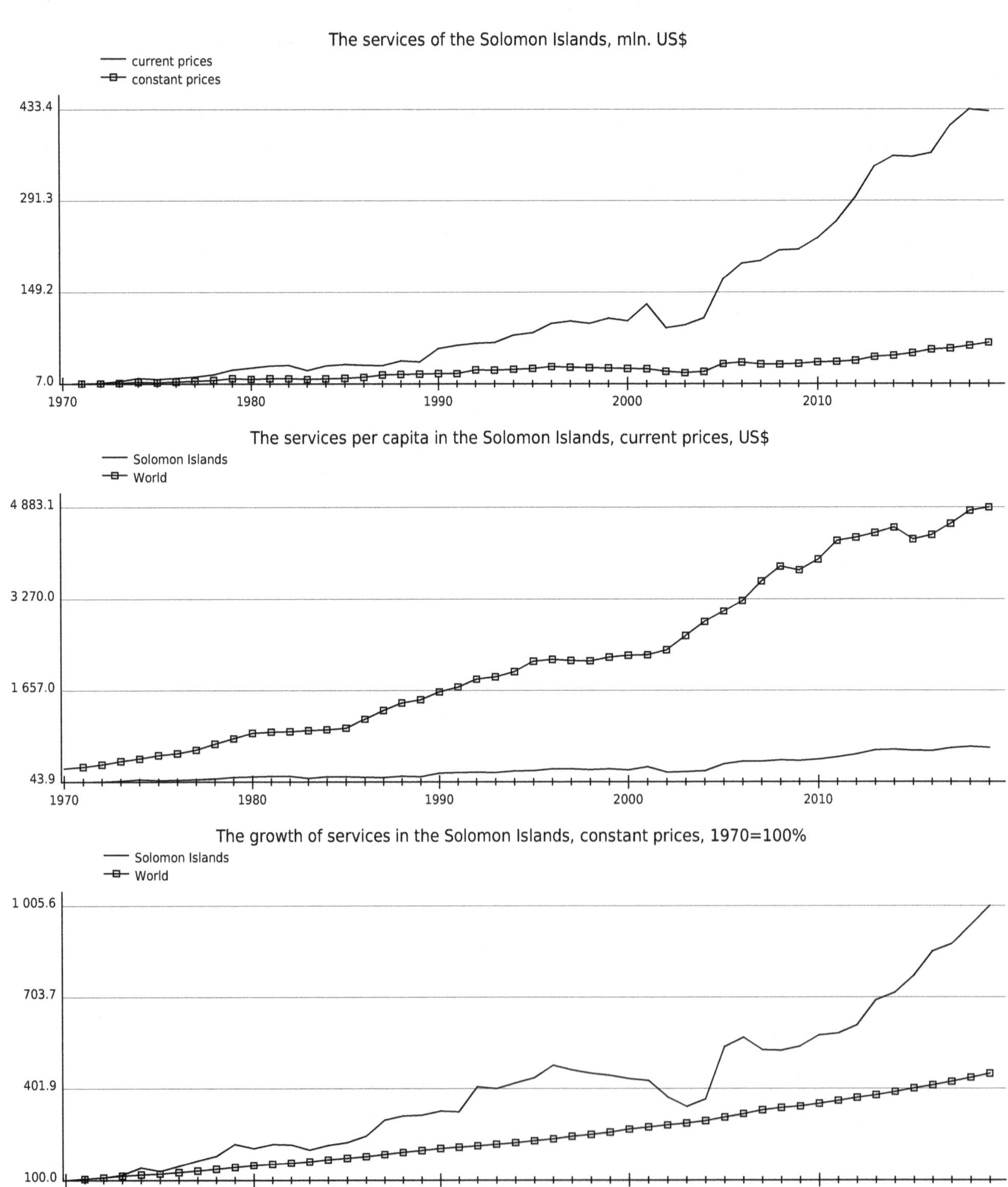

The services of the Solomon Islands, mln. US$

The services per capita in the Solomon Islands, current prices, US$

The growth of services in the Solomon Islands, constant prices, 1970=100%

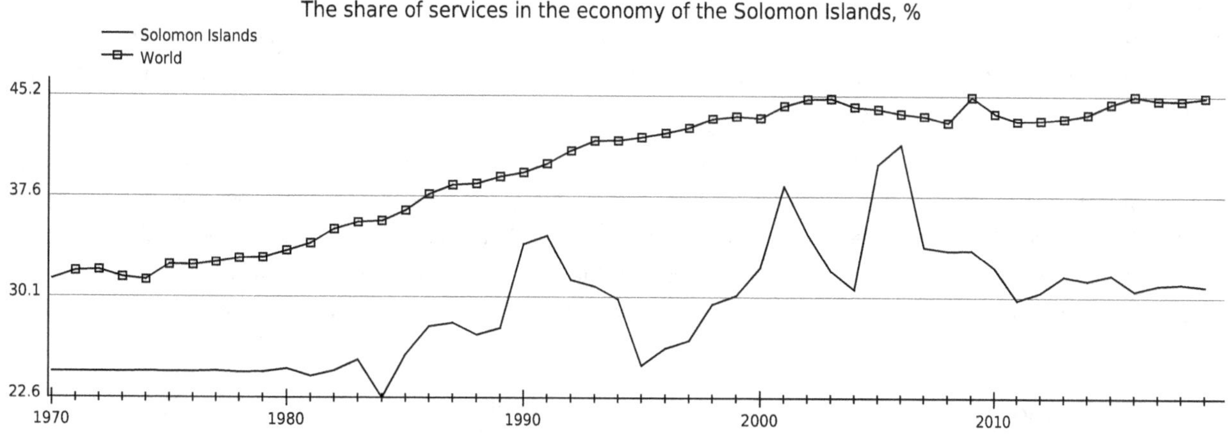

The 1970s

The Solomon Islands services were $14.8 million per year in the 1970s, ranked 169th in the world, and were on a par with Saint Vincent ($14.7 million). The share in the world was 0.0007%, and 0.038% in Oceania.

The share of services in the economy of the Solomon Islands was 24.5% in the 1970s, ranked 120th in the world, and was on a par with Southern Asia (24.5%), Eastern Asia (24.6%), Tonga (24.6%).

The Solomon Islands services per capita were $77.9 in the 1970s, ranked 144th in the world, and were on a par with Cabo Verde ($77.8), the Philippines ($76.1). The value added of services per capita in the Solomon Islands was less than services per capita in the world ($506.9) in 6.5 times, and was less than services per capita in Oceania ($1 847.3) in 23.7 times.

The growth of services in the Solomon Islands was 9.1% in the 1970s, ranked 25th in the world, and was on a par with Hong Kong (9.0%), Aruba (9.1%), Algeria (9.1%). The growth of services in the Solomon Islands (9.1%) was greater than growth of services in the world (4.1%), was greater than growth of services in Oceania (4.0%).

Comparison with neighbors. The value added of services in the Solomon Islands was greater than in Nauru ($8.9 million); but less than in Papua New Guinea ($763.7 million), in New Caledonia ($200.9 million), and in Vanuatu ($22.2 million). The Solomon Islands services per capita were less than in New Caledonia ($1 592.6), in Nauru ($1 248.5), in Papua New Guinea ($245.4), and in Vanuatu ($225.4). The growth of services in the Solomon Islands was greater than in Vanuatu (7.7%), in Papua New Guinea (3.1%), and in Nauru (1.1%); but less than in New Caledonia (9.1%).

Comparison with leaders. The services of the Solomon Islands were less than in the United States ($674.4 billion), in the USSR ($168.3 billion), in Japan ($153.8 billion), in Germany ($150.2 billion), and in France ($121.8 billion). The sector of services per capita in the Solomon Islands was less than in the USA ($3.1 thousand), in France ($2.3 thousand), in Germany ($1 907.6), in Japan ($1 381.3), and in the USSR ($667.3). The growth of services in the Solomon Islands was greater than in Japan (5.9%), in Germany (4.8%), in France (3.9%), in the USA (3.3%), and in the USSR (0.90%).

The 1980s

The value of services in the Solomon Islands was $35.8 million per year in the 1980s, ranked 171st in the world. The share in the world was 0.0007%, and 0.037% in Oceania.

The share of services in the economy of the Solomon Islands was 25.8% in the 1980s, ranked 119th in the world, and was on a par with Vietnam (25.8%), Mauritania (25.9%), the CAR (25.9%).

The services per capita in the Solomon Islands were $134.3 in the 1980s, ranked 140th in the world, and were on a par with the Philippines ($135.8), Kiribati ($132.2), Tanzania ($136.7). The value added of services per capita in the Solomon Islands was less than services per capita in the world ($1 115.5) in 8.3 times, and was less than services per capita in Oceania ($3 935.7) in 29.3 times.

The growth of services in the Solomon Islands was 3.7% in the 1980s, ranked 86th in the world, and was on a par with Mauritius (3.7%), Brazil (3.7%). The growth of services in the Solomon Islands (3.7%) was greater than growth of services in the world (3.3%), was less than growth of services in Oceania (4.0%).

Comparison with neighbors. The services of the Solomon Islands were greater than in Nauru ($12.0 million); but less than in Papua

New Guinea ($1.9 billion), in New Caledonia ($523.0 million), and in Vanuatu ($48.4 million). The services per capita in the Solomon Islands were less than in New Caledonia ($3.4 thousand), in Nauru ($1 422.1), in Papua New Guinea ($461.8), and in Vanuatu ($376.1). The growth of services in the Solomon Islands was greater than in Papua New Guinea (0.13%) and in Nauru (-2.4%); but less than in Vanuatu (4.9%) and in New Caledonia (4.0%).

Comparison with leaders. The value of services in the Solomon Islands was less than in the USA ($1.9 trillion), in Japan ($619.9 billion), in Germany ($362.2 billion), in France ($294.5 billion), and in the United Kingdom ($265.4 billion). The sector of services per capita in the Solomon Islands was less than in the USA ($7.8 thousand), in France ($5.2 thousand), in Japan ($5.1 thousand), in the United Kingdom ($4.7 thousand), and in Germany ($4.6 thousand). The growth of services in the Solomon Islands was greater than in the UK (3.3%), in Germany (3.1%), in the United States (2.8%), and in France (2.3%); but less than in Japan (4.8%).

The 1990s

The value added of services in the Solomon Islands was $85.3 million per year in the 1990s, ranked 189th in the world, and was on a par with Grenada ($84.0 million). The share in the world was 0.0007%, and 0.046% in Oceania.

The share of services in the economy of the Solomon Islands was 29.2% in the 1990s, ranked 121st in the world, and was on a par with Swaziland (29.3%), Lithuania (29.1%), Congo (29.1%).

The services per capita in the Solomon Islands were $240.1 in the 1990s, ranked 141st in the world, and were on a par with Ukraine ($241.9), Cameroon ($242.4), Bolivia ($237.1). The sector of services per capita in the Solomon Islands was less than services per capita in the world ($2 014.6) in 8.4 times, and was less than services per capita in Oceania ($6 423.5) in 26.8 times.

The growth of services in the Solomon Islands was 3.5% in the 1990s, ranked 78th in the world, and was on a par with Eswatini (3.5%), Brunei (3.6%). The growth of services in the Solomon Islands (3.5%) was greater than growth of services in the world (2.7%), was less than growth of services in Oceania (3.6%).

Comparison with neighbors. The value added of services in the Solomon Islands was greater than in Vanuatu ($75.3 million) and in Nauru ($11.1 million); but less than in Papua New Guinea ($2.1 billion) and in New Caledonia ($1.5 billion). The value added of services per capita in the Solomon Islands was less than in New Caledonia ($8.0 thousand), in Nauru ($1 078.8), in Vanuatu ($456.0), and in Papua New Guinea ($400.6). The growth of services in the Solomon Islands was greater than in Papua New Guinea (2.9%), in Vanuatu (0.86%), and in Nauru (-13.3%); but less than in New Caledonia (5.2%).

Comparison with leaders. The value of services in the Solomon Islands was less than in the United States ($3.8 trillion), in Japan ($1.6 trillion), in Germany ($908.0 billion), in France ($628.2 billion), and in the United Kingdom ($592.3 billion). The value of services per capita in the Solomon Islands was less than in the USA ($14.4 thousand), in Japan ($12.8 thousand), in Germany ($11.3 thousand), in France ($10.6 thousand), and in the United Kingdom ($10.2 thousand). The growth of services in the Solomon Islands was greater than in Germany (3.2%), in the UK (3.0%), in the United States (2.3%), in Japan (1.7%), and in France (1.6%).

The 2000s

The value of services in the Solomon Islands was $152.9 million per year in the 2000s, ranked 194th in the world. The share in the world was 0.0008%, and 0.041% in Oceania.

The share of services in the economy of the Solomon Islands was 35.1% in the 2000s, ranked 101st in the world, and was on a par with Czechia (35.1%), Botswana (35.1%), Lesotho (35.3%).

The sector of services per capita in the Solomon Islands was $329.6 in the 2000s, ranked 149th in the world. The value added of services per capita in the Solomon Islands was less than services per capita in the world ($3 011.2) in 9.1 times, and was less than services per capita in Oceania ($11 122.0) in 33.7 times.

The growth of services in the Solomon Islands was 2% in the 2000s, ranked 171st in the world, and was on a par with Croatia (2.0%), the United States (2.0%). The growth of services in the Solomon Islands (2.0%) was less than growth of services in the world (2.9%), was less than growth of services in Oceania (3.2%).

Comparison with neighbors. The Solomon Islands services were greater than in Vanuatu ($129.9 million) and in Nauru ($10.5 million); but less than in New Caledonia ($2.9 billion) and in Papua New Guinea ($1.9 billion). The sector of services per capita in the Solomon Islands was greater than in Papua New Guinea ($299.2); but less than in New Caledonia ($12.3 thousand), in Nauru ($1 051.8), and in Vanuatu ($627.5). The growth of services in the Solomon Islands was greater than in Papua New Guinea (1.5%) and in Nauru

(-3.0%); but less than in New Caledonia (3.3%) and in Vanuatu (2.9%).

Comparison with leaders. The sector of services in the Solomon Islands was less than in the USA ($6.7 trillion), in Japan ($2.0 trillion), in Germany ($1.2 trillion), in the UK ($1.1 trillion), and in France ($997.0 billion). The sector of services per capita in the Solomon Islands was less than in the United States ($22.9 thousand), in the United Kingdom ($18.0 thousand), in France ($15.9 thousand), in Japan ($15.3 thousand), and in Germany ($15.0 thousand). The growth of services in the Solomon Islands was greater than in France (1.5%), in Japan (1.2%), and in Germany (0.57%); but less than in the United Kingdom (2.7%) and in the United States (2.0%).

The 2010s

The sector of services in the Solomon Islands was $349.2 million per year in the 2010s, ranked 190th in the world. The share in the world was 0.0011%, and 0.044% in Oceania.

The share of services in the economy of the Solomon Islands was 31.1% in the 2010s, ranked 136th in the world, and was on a par with North Korea (31.3%).

The sector of services per capita in the Solomon Islands was $585.5 in the 2010s, ranked 154th in the world, and was on a par with Nigeria ($578.2). The sector of services per capita in the Solomon Islands was less than services per capita in the world ($4 467.8) in 7.6 times, and was less than services per capita in Oceania ($20 232.3) in 34.6 times.

The growth of services in the Solomon Islands was 6.4% in the 2010s, ranked 26th in the world, and was on a par with Cambodia (6.4%). The growth of services in the Solomon Islands (6.4%) was greater than growth of services in the world (2.7%), was greater than growth of services in Oceania (2.9%).

Comparison with neighbors. The value added of services in the Solomon Islands was 42.9% higher than in Vanuatu ($244.4 million) and 15.5 times higher than in Nauru ($22.6 million); but 17.3 times lower than in Papua New Guinea ($6.1 billion) and 13.7 times lower than in New Caledonia ($4.8 billion). The sector of services per capita in the Solomon Islands was 30.4 times lower than in New Caledonia ($17.8 thousand), 3.7 times lower than in Nauru ($2.2 thousand), 35.9% lower than in Vanuatu ($913.3), and 22.3% lower than in Papua New Guinea ($753.7). The growth of services in the Solomon Islands was greater than in Papua New Guinea (5.0%), in New Caledonia (3.1%), and in Vanuatu (2.3%); but less than in Nauru (8.3%).

Comparison with leaders. The services of the Solomon Islands were 28 505.3 times lower than in the USA ($10.0 trillion), 10 156.5 times lower than in China ($3.5 trillion), 6 509.9 times lower than in Japan ($2.3 trillion), 4 602.8 times lower than in Germany ($1.6 trillion), and 3 881.3 times lower than in the UK ($1.4 trillion). The value of services per capita in the Solomon Islands was 53.2 times lower than in the USA ($31.2 thousand), 35.3 times lower than in the UK ($20.7 thousand), 33.5 times lower than in Germany ($19.6 thousand), 30.4 times lower than in Japan ($17.8 thousand), and 4.3 times lower than in China ($2.5 thousand). The growth of services in the Solomon Islands was greater than in the United States (1.8%), in the UK (1.7%), in Germany (1.2%), and in Japan (0.99%); but less than in China (8.4%).

Part III. External relations

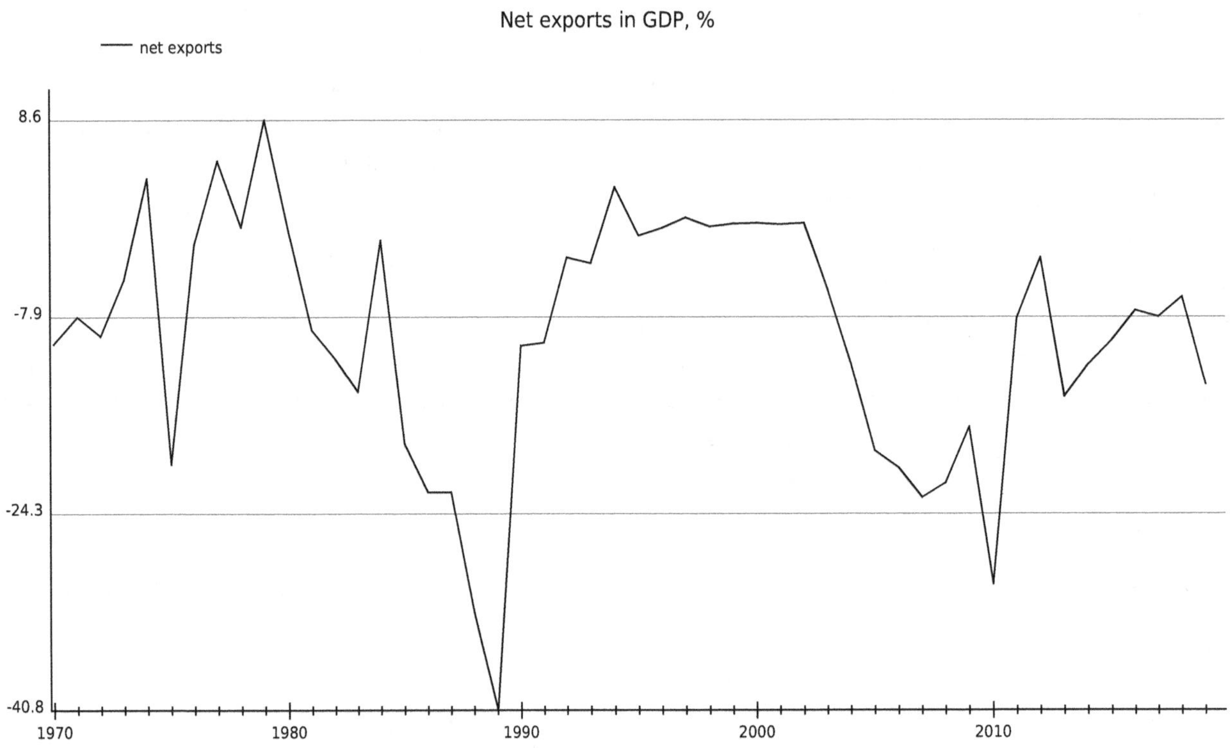

Chapter X. Exports

Exports of goods and services

The exports of the Solomon Islands grew up from $24.6 million per year in the 1970s to $573.0 million per year in the 2010s, that is by $548.4 million or 23.3 times. The change occurred at $415.5 million due to a 3.6-fold increase in prices, as also at $80.4 million due to a 2.0-fold increase in per capita rate, as well as at $52.5 million due to the rise in population. The average annual growth in exports is 5.7%. The minimum value of exports was in 1970 at $8.0 million. The maximum value of exports was in 2018 at $702.9 million.

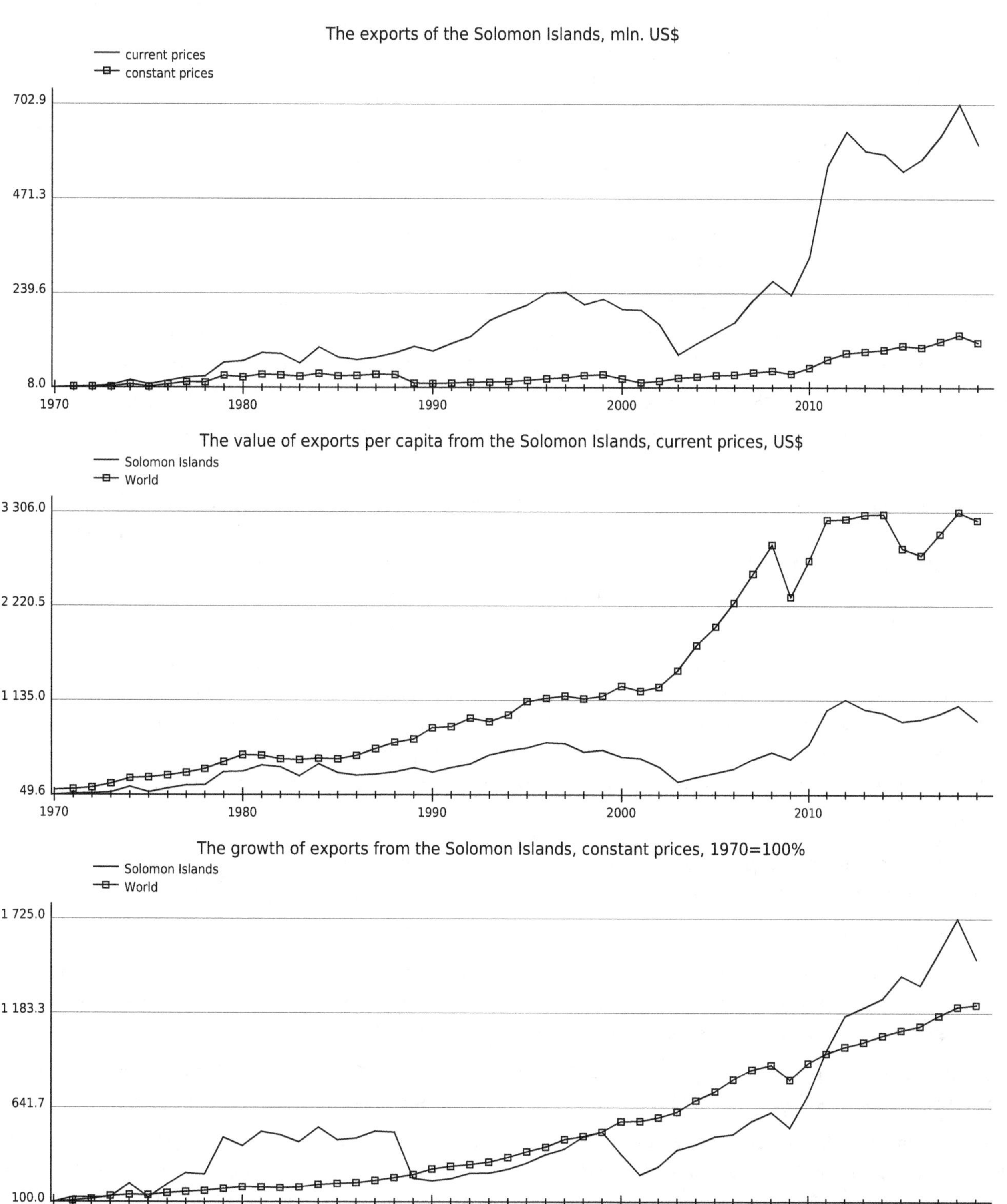

The exports of the Solomon Islands, mln. US$

The value of exports per capita from the Solomon Islands, current prices, US$

The growth of exports from the Solomon Islands, constant prices, 1970=100%

The 1970s

The value of exports from the Solomon Islands was $24.6 million per year in the 1970s, ranked 159th in the world. The share in the world was 0.0025%, and 0.13% from Oceania.

The share of exports in GDP of the Solomon Islands was 36.5% in the 1970s, ranked 67th in the world, and was on a par with Cabo Verde (36.4%), Norway (36.7%), Togo (36.9%).

The value of exports per capita from the Solomon Islands was $129.3 in the 1970s, ranked 124th in the world, and was on a par with Mexico ($130.3), DR Congo ($130.6), Saint Vincent and the Grenadines ($132.2). The Solomon Islands exports per capita were less than exports per capita in the world ($242.1) by 46.6%, and were less than exports per capita from Oceania ($882.5) in 6.8 times.

The growth of exports from the Solomon Islands was 18.8% in the 1970s, ranked 6th in the world. The growth of exports from the Solomon Islands (18.8%) was greater than growth of exports in the world (6.5%), was greater than growth of exports from Oceania (4.4%).

Comparison with neighbors. The value of exports from the Solomon Islands was greater than from Nauru ($16.7 million); but less than from Papua New Guinea ($929.0 million), from New Caledonia ($270.2 million), and from Vanuatu ($37.2 million). The exports per capita from the Solomon Islands were less than from Nauru ($2.4 thousand), from New Caledonia ($2.1 thousand), from Vanuatu ($377.3), and from Papua New Guinea ($298.5). The growth of exports from the Solomon Islands was greater than from Papua New Guinea (10.8%), from Vanuatu (7.7%), from Nauru (1.9%), and from New Caledonia (-1.9%).

Comparison with leaders. The exports of the Solomon Islands were less than from the United States ($128.0 billion), from Germany ($82.9 billion), from France ($64.3 billion), from Japan ($64.1 billion), and from the UK ($61.3 billion). The value of exports per capita from the Solomon Islands was less than from France ($1 199.1), from the United Kingdom ($1 094.1), from Germany ($1 052.2), from the United States ($586.5), and from Japan ($575.8). The growth of exports from the Solomon Islands was greater than from Japan (8.6%), from France (7.8%), from the USA (6.8%), from Germany (5.1%), and from the United Kingdom (5.0%).

The 1980s

The value of exports from the Solomon Islands was $87.1 million per year in the 1980s, ranked 156th in the world. The share in the world was 0.0034%, and 0.20% from Oceania.

The share of exports in GDP of the Solomon Islands was 55.8% in the 1980s, ranked 28th in the world.

The value of exports per capita from the Solomon Islands was $326.5 in the 1980s, ranked 105th in the world, and was on a par with Côte d'Ivoire ($325.1), Djibouti ($331.4). The value of exports per capita from the Solomon Islands was less than exports per capita in the world ($529.9) by 38.4%, and was less than exports per capita from Oceania ($1 779.0) in 5.4 times.

The growth of exports from the Solomon Islands was -6.7% in the 1980s, ranked 179th in the world. The growth of exports from the Solomon Islands (-6.7%) was less than growth of exports in the world (3.8%), was less than growth of exports from Oceania (4.3%).

Comparison with neighbors. The Solomon Islands exports were greater than from Vanuatu ($62.7 million) and from Nauru ($7.8 million); but less than from Papua New Guinea ($1.9 billion) and from New Caledonia ($362.4 million). The Solomon Islands exports per capita were less than from New Caledonia ($2.3 thousand), from Nauru ($919.2), from Vanuatu ($486.7), and from Papua New

Guinea ($463.9). The growth of exports from the Solomon Islands was greater than from Nauru (-13.4%); but less than from Papua New Guinea (3.0%), from New Caledonia (2.8%), and from Vanuatu (1.5%).

Comparison with leaders. The Solomon Islands exports were less than from the USA ($338.6 billion), from Japan ($210.6 billion), from Germany ($208.1 billion), from France ($155.9 billion), and from the UK ($155.0 billion). The exports per capita from the Solomon Islands were less than from France ($2.8 thousand), from the United Kingdom ($2.7 thousand), from Germany ($2.7 thousand), from Japan ($1 736.5), and from the United States ($1 413.8). The growth of exports from the Solomon Islands was less than from Japan (6.7%), from the United States (5.7%), from Germany (4.7%), from France (4.0%), and from the UK (3.0%).

The 1990s

The value of exports from the Solomon Islands was $184.0 million per year in the 1990s, ranked 179th in the world, and was on a par with Lesotho ($181.2 million). The share in the world was 0.0031%, and 0.20% from Oceania.

The share of exports in GDP of the Solomon Islands was 57.4% in the 1990s, ranked 30th in the world.

The value of exports per capita from the Solomon Islands was $517.8 in the 1990s, ranked 112th in the world, and was on a par with Angola ($526.3), Equatorial Guinea ($508.4), Congo ($505.7). The value of exports per capita from the Solomon Islands was less than exports per capita in the world ($1 029.5) by 49.7%, and was less than exports per capita from Oceania ($3 150.8) in 6.1 times.

The growth of exports from the Solomon Islands was 7.9% in the 1990s, ranked 54th in the world, and was on a par with Hong Kong (7.8%), Andorra (7.9%), Australia (7.9%). The growth of exports from the Solomon Islands (7.9%) was greater than growth of exports in the world (6.9%), was greater than growth of exports from Oceania (7.2%).

Comparison with neighbors. The Solomon Islands exports were greater than from Vanuatu ($111.4 million) and from Nauru ($5.2 million); but less than from Papua New Guinea ($3.5 billion) and from New Caledonia ($580.4 million). The value of exports per capita from the Solomon Islands was greater than from Nauru ($503.7); but less than from New Caledonia ($3.0 thousand), from Papua New Guinea ($687.8), and from Vanuatu ($675.1). The growth of exports from the Solomon Islands was greater than from Papua New Guinea (5.4%), from Vanuatu (3.2%), from New Caledonia (-3.3%), and from Nauru (-14.3%).

Comparison with leaders. The value of exports from the Solomon Islands was less than from the United States ($773.6 billion), from Germany ($509.0 billion), from Japan ($418.7 billion), from France ($329.8 billion), and from the United Kingdom ($324.3 billion). The Solomon Islands exports per capita were less than from Germany ($6.3 thousand), from the United Kingdom ($5.6 thousand), from France ($5.6 thousand), from Japan ($3.3 thousand), and from the United States ($2.9 thousand). The growth of exports from the Solomon Islands was greater than from the United States (7.2%), from France (6.5%), from Germany (6.0%), from the United Kingdom (5.7%), and from Japan (4.2%).

The 2000s

The exports of the Solomon Islands were $180.0 million per year in the 2000s, ranked 190th in the world, and were on a par with Vanuatu ($175.6 million). The share in the world was 0.0014%, and 0.098% from Oceania.

The structure of exports: primary products (18.7%) and resource-based manufactures (79.2%).

The Solomon Islands exported goods to China (42.2%), South Korea (10.6%), Japan (8.1%), Thailand (7.1%), the Philippines (6.8%) and other countries (25.2%).

The share of exports in GDP of the Solomon Islands was 41.0% in the 2000s, ranked 85th in the world, and was on a par with Finland (40.7%), Bhutan (41.4%).

The value of exports per capita from the Solomon Islands was $387.9 in the 2000s, ranked 153rd in the world, and was on a par with Tonga ($391.8), Djibouti ($383.2), Sri Lanka ($397.3). The Solomon Islands exports per capita were less than exports per capita in the world ($1 933.7) in 5.0 times, and were less than exports per capita from Oceania ($5 498.6) in 14.2 times.

The growth of exports from the Solomon Islands was 0.5% in the 2000s, ranked 182nd in the world. The growth of exports from the Solomon Islands (0.46%) was less than growth of exports in the world (4.8%), was less than growth of exports from Oceania (3.0%).

Comparison with neighbors. The value of exports from the Solomon Islands was greater than from Vanuatu ($175.6 million) and from Nauru ($4.1 million); but less than from Papua New Guinea ($5.3 billion) and from New Caledonia ($1.3 billion). The Solomon Islands exports per capita were less than from New Caledonia ($5.5 thousand), from Vanuatu ($848.6), from Papua New Guinea ($822.7), and from Nauru ($407.7). The growth of exports from the Solomon Islands was greater than from Nauru (0.24%); but less than from Vanuatu (7.9%), from Papua New Guinea (3.1%), and from New Caledonia (1.4%).

Comparison with leaders. The value of exports from the Solomon Islands was less than from the USA ($1.3 trillion), from Germany ($1.0 trillion), from China ($780.2 billion), from Japan ($626.3 billion), and from the UK ($591.1 billion). The Solomon Islands exports per capita were less than from Germany ($12.8 thousand), from the United Kingdom ($9.8 thousand), from Japan ($4.9 thousand), from the United States ($4.5 thousand), and from China ($588.1). The growth of exports from the Solomon Islands was less than from China (12.7%), from Germany (5.0%), from Japan (3.5%), from the United States (3.3%), and from the United Kingdom (2.8%).

The 2010s

The value of exports from the Solomon Islands was $573.0 million per year in the 2010s, ranked 186th in the world, and was on a par with Antigua and Barbuda ($573.2 million). The share in the world was 0.0025%, and 0.15% from Oceania.

The structure of exports: primary products (8.5%) and resource-based manufactures (82.4%).

The Solomon Islands exported goods to China (61.0%), Australia (7.2%), Italy (5.4%), India (3.8%), Thailand (3.0%) and other countries (19.6%).

The share of exports in GDP of the Solomon Islands was 53.4% in the 2010s, ranked 52nd in the world, and was on a par with Palau (53.2%), Austria (53.7%).

The value of exports per capita from the Solomon Islands was $960.5 in the 2010s, ranked 145th in the world, and was on a par with Kosovo ($955.0). The value of exports per capita from the Solomon Islands was less than exports per capita in the world ($3 098.9) in 3.2 times, and was less than exports per capita from Oceania ($9 599.0) in 10.0 times.

The growth of exports from the Solomon Islands was 11% in the 2010s, ranked 18th in the world. The growth of exports from the Solomon Islands (11.0%) was greater than growth of exports in the world (4.4%), was greater than growth of exports from Oceania (3.9%).

Comparison with neighbors. The value of exports from the Solomon Islands was 44.8% higher than from Vanuatu ($395.6 million) and 37.3 times higher than from Nauru ($15.4 million); but 19.6 times lower than from Papua New Guinea ($11.2 billion) and 3.1 times lower than from New Caledonia ($1.8 billion). The exports per capita from the Solomon Islands were 6.8 times lower than from New Caledonia ($6.6 thousand), 35.2% lower than from Nauru ($1 483.3), 35.0% lower than from Vanuatu ($1 478.1), and 31.2% lower than from Papua New Guinea ($1 395.6). The growth of exports from the Solomon Islands was greater than from Nauru (5.8%), from Vanuatu (4.0%), from New Caledonia (3.9%), and from Papua New Guinea (3.5%).

Comparison with leaders. The exports of the Solomon Islands were 4 002.5 times lower than from China ($2.3 trillion), 3 961.2 times lower than from the United States ($2.3 trillion), 2 937.7 times lower than from Germany ($1.7 trillion), 1 499.9 times lower than from Japan ($859.4 billion), and 1 422.5 times lower than from the United Kingdom ($815.1 billion). The value of exports per capita from the Solomon Islands was 21.4 times lower than from Germany ($20.6 thousand), 12.9 times lower than from the United Kingdom ($12.4 thousand), 7.4 times lower than from the USA ($7.1 thousand), 7.0 times lower than from Japan ($6.7 thousand), and 41.3% lower than from China ($1 635.3). The growth of exports from the Solomon Islands was greater than from China (6.8%), from Germany (4.7%), from Japan (4.6%), from the USA (3.7%), and from the United Kingdom (3.1%).

Chapter XI. Imports

Imports of goods and services

The imports of the Solomon Islands rose from $25.5 million per year in the 1970s to $687.0 million per year in the 2010s, that is by $661.5 million or 27.0 times. The change occurred at $535.6 million due to a 4.5-fold increase in prices, as also at $71.6 million due to a 1.9-fold increase in per capita rate, as well as at $54.3 million due to the rise in population. The average annual growth in imports is 5.0%. The minimum value of imports was in 1970 at $11.2 million. The maximum value of imports was in 2018 at $784.0 million.

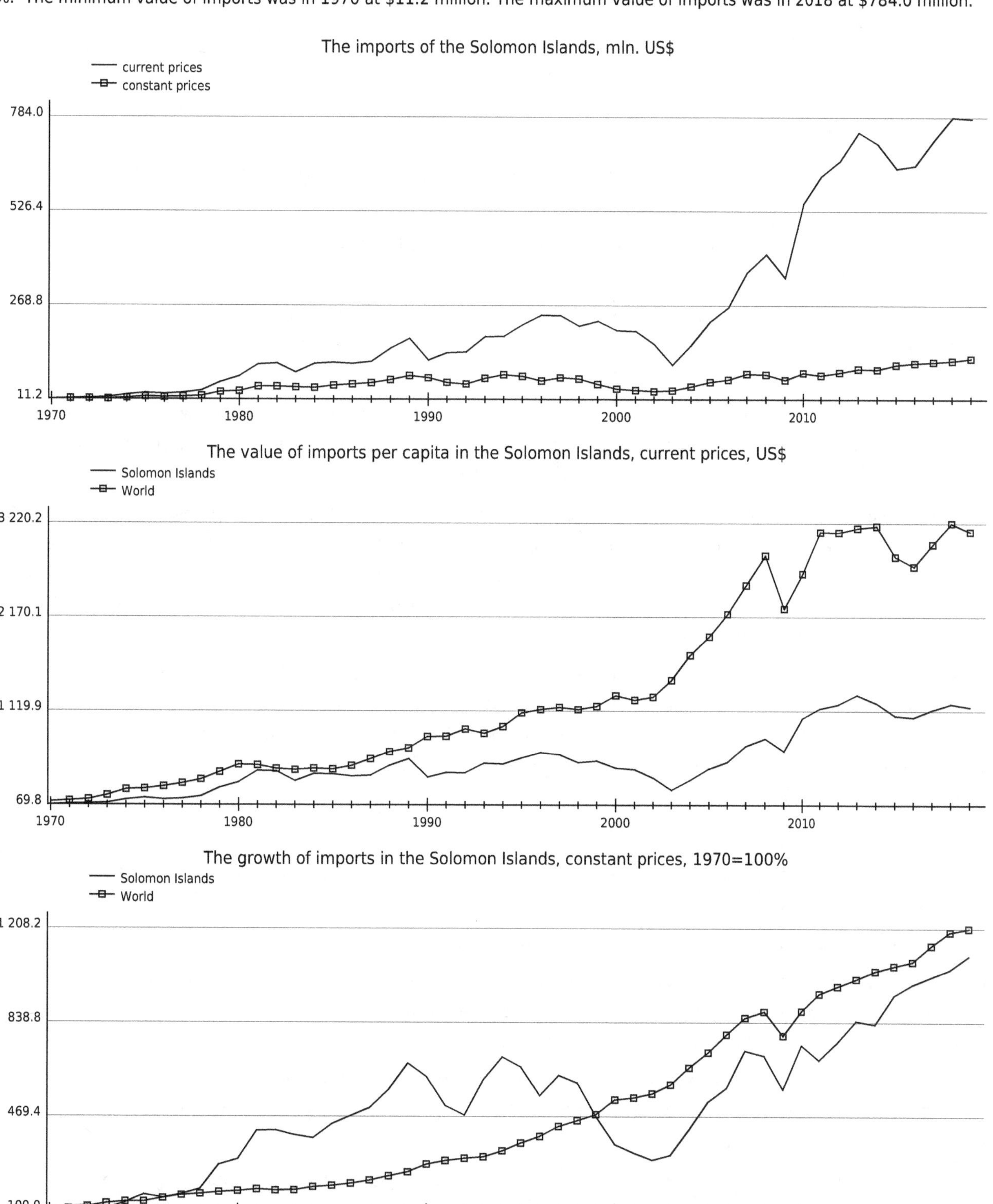

The imports of the Solomon Islands, mln. US$

The value of imports per capita in the Solomon Islands, current prices, US$

The growth of imports in the Solomon Islands, constant prices, 1970=100%

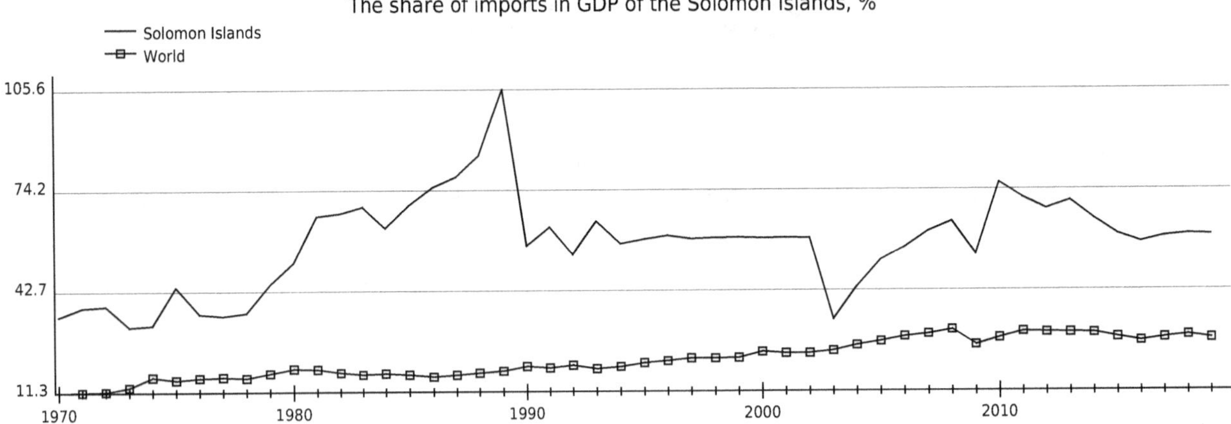

The 1970s

The imports of the Solomon Islands were $25.5 million per year in the 1970s, ranked 167th in the world, and were on a par with Grenada ($25.5 million), Saint Kitts and Nevis ($25.8 million). The share in the world was 0.0026%, and 0.13% in Oceania.

The share of imports in GDP of the Solomon Islands was 37.8% in the 1970s, ranked 84th in the world, and was on a par with Kiribati (37.8%), Bulgaria (37.9%).

The Solomon Islands imports per capita were $133.8 in the 1970s, ranked 133rd in the world, and were on a par with Togo ($135.5). The value of imports per capita in the Solomon Islands was less than imports per capita in the world ($244.3) by 45.2%, and was less than imports per capita in Oceania ($913.9) in 6.8 times.

The growth of imports in the Solomon Islands was 12.1% in the 1970s, ranked 19th in the world, and was on a par with Malaysia (12.0%), Iran (12.1%), Western Asia (12.1%). The growth of imports in the Solomon Islands (12.1%) was greater than growth of imports in the world (6.3%), was greater than growth of imports in Oceania (2.8%).

Comparison with neighbors. The imports of the Solomon Islands were greater than in Nauru ($11.2 million); but less than in Papua New Guinea ($934.3 million), in New Caledonia ($289.4 million), and in Vanuatu ($52.1 million). The value of imports per capita in the Solomon Islands was less than in New Caledonia ($2.3 thousand), in Nauru ($1 582.5), in Vanuatu ($528.9), and in Papua New Guinea ($300.2). The growth of imports in the Solomon Islands was greater than in Vanuatu (7.7%), in Nauru (4.3%), in Papua New Guinea (-0.29%), and in New Caledonia (-4.4%).

Comparison with leaders. The Solomon Islands imports were less than in the United States ($133.2 billion), in Germany ($92.5 billion), in France ($63.3 billion), in the United Kingdom ($62.4 billion), and in Japan ($61.0 billion). The value of imports per capita in the Solomon Islands was less than in France ($1 181.1), in Germany ($1 175.1), in the United Kingdom ($1 113.2), in the United States ($610.4), and in Japan ($547.6). The growth of imports in the Solomon Islands was greater than in France (7.2%), in Japan (7.0%), in Germany (5.6%), in the USA (5.1%), and in the UK (4.5%).

The 1980s

The value of imports in the Solomon Islands was $114.6 million per year in the 1980s, ranked 160th in the world. The share in the world was 0.0044%, and 0.23% in Oceania.

The share of imports in GDP of the Solomon Islands was 73.4% in the 1980s, ranked 26th in the world.

The imports per capita in the Solomon Islands were $429.7 in the 1980s, ranked 109th in the world, and were on a par with Samoa ($434.5), Iran ($439.2). The Solomon Islands imports per capita were less than imports per capita in the world ($539.1) by 20.3%, and were less than imports per capita in Oceania ($1 987.8) in 4.6 times.

The growth of imports in the Solomon Islands was 9.2% in the 1980s, ranked 15th in the world, and was on a par with Thailand (9.2%), Malaysia (9.2%). The growth of imports in the Solomon Islands (9.2%) was greater than growth of imports in the world (3.8%), was greater than growth of imports in Oceania (5.7%).

Comparison with neighbors. The value of imports in the Solomon Islands was greater than in Vanuatu ($91.1 million) and in Nauru ($46.4 million); but less than in Papua New Guinea ($2.1 billion) and in New Caledonia ($464.6 million). The Solomon Islands imports per capita were less than in Nauru ($5.5 thousand), in New Caledonia ($3.0 thousand), in Vanuatu ($707.1), and in Papua New Guinea ($532.2). The growth of imports in the Solomon Islands was greater than in Nauru (5.4%), in New Caledonia (3.8%), in Vanuatu (2.9%), and in Papua New Guinea (0.31%).

Comparison with leaders. The imports of the Solomon Islands were less than in the United States ($417.2 billion), in Germany ($225.6 billion), in Japan ($175.9 billion), in France ($162.0 billion), and in the United Kingdom ($157.7 billion). The imports per capita in the Solomon Islands were less than in Germany ($2.9 thousand), in France ($2.9 thousand), in the United Kingdom ($2.8 thousand), in the United States ($1 742.4), and in Japan ($1 450.4). The growth of imports in the Solomon Islands was greater than in the United States (5.8%), in the UK (5.1%), in Japan (4.6%), in France (4.3%), and in Germany (3.3%).

The 1990s

The value of imports in the Solomon Islands was $189.6 million per year in the 1990s, ranked 187th in the world, and was on a par with the Comoros ($192.7 million). The share in the world was 0.0033%, and 0.20% in Oceania.

The share of imports in GDP of the Solomon Islands was 59.1% in the 1990s, ranked 45th in the world, and was on a par with Greenland (59.0%), the Turks and Caicos Islands (58.8%), Belize (58.8%).

The imports per capita in the Solomon Islands were $533.5 in the 1990s, ranked 128th in the world, and were on a par with Bulgaria ($534.4). The imports per capita in the Solomon Islands were less than imports per capita in the world ($1 015.5) by 47.5%, and were less than imports per capita in Oceania ($3 244.3) in 6.1 times.

The growth of imports in the Solomon Islands was -3.6% in the 1990s, ranked 185th in the world, and was on a par with Armenia (-3.6%). The growth of imports in the Solomon Islands (-3.6%) was less than growth of imports in the world (6.6%), was less than growth of imports in Oceania (6.2%).

Comparison with neighbors. The Solomon Islands imports were greater than in Vanuatu ($135.7 million) and in Nauru ($28.2 million); but less than in Papua New Guinea ($3.0 billion) and in New Caledonia ($1.1 billion). The value of imports per capita in the Solomon Islands was less than in New Caledonia ($6.0 thousand), in Nauru ($2.7 thousand), in Vanuatu ($822.4), and in Papua New Guinea ($582.4). The growth of imports in the Solomon Islands was greater than in Nauru (-18.0%); but less than in Papua New Guinea (3.5%), in New Caledonia (3.1%), and in Vanuatu (2.0%).

Comparison with leaders. The value of imports in the Solomon Islands was less than in the USA ($874.1 billion), in Germany ($501.6 billion), in Japan ($355.9 billion), in the UK ($330.2 billion), and in France ($308.5 billion). The value of imports per capita in the Solomon Islands was less than in Germany ($6.2 thousand), in the United Kingdom ($5.7 thousand), in France ($5.2 thousand), in the United States ($3.3 thousand), and in Japan ($2.8 thousand). The growth of imports in the Solomon Islands was less than in the United States (8.3%), in Germany (6.4%), in France (5.1%), in the UK (5.1%), and in Japan (3.3%).

The 2000s

The imports of the Solomon Islands were $242.3 million per year in the 2000s, ranked 193rd in the world, and were on a par with Samoa ($237.9 million). The share in the world was 0.0020%, and 0.12% in Oceania.

The structure of imports: primary products (8.7%), resource-based manufactures (38.2%), low technology manufactures (11.6%), medium technology manufactures (22.7%), and high technology manufactures (8.5%).

The Solomon Islands imported goods from Singapore (31.3%), Australia (27.7%), Papua New Guinea (5.7%), New Zealand (5.6%), Japan (4.7%) and other countries (25.1%).

The share of imports in GDP of the Solomon Islands was 55.2% in the 2000s, ranked 70th in the world, and was on a par with Greenland (55.5%), Tonga (54.9%), Samoa (54.8%).

The imports per capita in the Solomon Islands were $522.2 in the 2000s, ranked 155th in the world, and were on a par with Sri Lanka ($519.1), Vietnam ($517.1). The Solomon Islands imports per capita were less than imports per capita in the world ($1 899.9) in 3.6 times, and were less than imports per capita in Oceania ($5 844.4) in 11.2 times.

The growth of imports in the Solomon Islands was 2.1% in the 2000s, ranked 172nd in the world, and was on a par with Portugal (2.0%). The growth of imports in the Solomon Islands (2.1%) was less than growth of imports in the world (5.1%), was less than growth of imports in Oceania (6.6%).

Comparison with neighbors. The value of imports in the Solomon Islands was greater than in Vanuatu ($209.9 million) and in Nauru ($26.2 million); but less than in Papua New Guinea ($4.2 billion) and in New Caledonia ($2.6 billion). The imports per capita in the Solomon Islands were less than in New Caledonia ($11.0 thousand), in Nauru ($2.6 thousand), in Vanuatu ($1 014.3), and in Papua New Guinea ($648.5). The growth of imports in the Solomon Islands was less than in Vanuatu (5.9%), in Papua New Guinea (5.4%), in New Caledonia (3.9%), and in Nauru (3.5%).

Comparison with leaders. The imports of the Solomon Islands were less than in the USA ($1.9 trillion), in Germany ($914.7 billion), in the United Kingdom ($641.8 billion), in China ($641.1 billion), and in Japan ($566.4 billion). The imports per capita in the Solomon Islands were greater than in China ($483.3); but less than in Germany ($11.2 thousand), in the United Kingdom ($10.6 thousand), in the United States ($6.4 thousand), and in Japan ($4.4 thousand). The growth of imports in the Solomon Islands was greater than in Japan (1.8%); but less than in China (15.1%), in Germany (3.7%), in the UK (3.1%), and in the USA (2.8%).

The 2010s

The value of imports in the Solomon Islands was $687.0 million per year in the 2010s, ranked 187th in the world, and was on a par with the Central African Republic ($682.0 million). The share in the world was 0.0031%, and 0.18% in Oceania.

The structure of imports: primary products (11.3%), resource-based manufactures (34.0%), low technology manufactures (12.8%), medium technology manufactures (24.5%), and high technology manufactures (8.0%).

The Solomon Islands imported goods from Singapore (23.3%), Australia (23.0%), China (13.6%), Malaysia (6.3%), New Zealand (5.1%) and other countries (28.7%).

The share of imports in GDP of the Solomon Islands was 64.0% in the 2010s, ranked 43rd in the world, and was on a par with Cambodia (64.0%), Montenegro (63.7%), Malaysia (64.3%).

The value of imports per capita in the Solomon Islands was $1 151.7 in the 2010s, ranked 152nd in the world, and was on a par with Guatemala ($1 162.8), Cuba ($1 163.9). The Solomon Islands imports per capita were less than imports per capita in the world ($3 015.6) in 2.6 times, and were less than imports per capita in Oceania ($9 570.0) in 8.3 times.

The growth of imports in the Solomon Islands was 6.7% in the 2010s, ranked 43rd in the world, and was on a par with Oman (6.7%). The growth of imports in the Solomon Islands (6.7%) was greater than growth of imports in the world (4.4%), was greater than growth of imports in Oceania (5.7%).

Comparison with neighbors. The Solomon Islands imports were 51.1% higher than in Vanuatu ($454.7 million) and 6.3 times higher than in Nauru ($108.6 million); but 15.2 times lower than in Papua New Guinea ($10.4 billion) and 6.1 times lower than in New Caledonia ($4.2 billion). The Solomon Islands imports per capita were 13.6 times lower than in New Caledonia ($15.7 thousand), 9.1 times lower than in Nauru ($10.5 thousand), 32.2% lower than in Vanuatu ($1 698.9), and 11.3% lower than in Papua New Guinea ($1 298.9). The growth of imports in the Solomon Islands was greater than in Papua New Guinea (4.5%), in Vanuatu (3.8%), and in New Caledonia (1.6%); but less than in Nauru (10.3%).

Comparison with leaders. The imports of the Solomon Islands were 4 100.6 times lower than in the United States ($2.8 trillion), 3 011.7 times lower than in China ($2.1 trillion), 2 117.4 times lower than in Germany ($1.5 trillion), 1 277.9 times lower than in Japan ($877.9 billion), and 1 244.2 times lower than in the United Kingdom ($854.8 billion). The Solomon Islands imports per capita were 15.4 times lower than in Germany ($17.8 thousand), 11.3 times lower than in the United Kingdom ($13.0 thousand), 7.7 times lower than in the United States ($8.8 thousand), 6.0 times lower than in Japan ($6.9 thousand), and 21.9% lower than in China ($1 475.4). The growth of imports in the Solomon Islands was greater than in Germany (4.8%), in the United States (4.4%), in Japan (3.8%), and in the UK (3.6%); but less than in China (8.2%).

Part IV. Consumption

Chapter XII. Government consumption expenditure

General government final consumption expenditure

The government expenditure of the Solomon Islands increased from $15.5 million per year in the 1970s to $337.3 million per year in the 2010s, that is by $321.7 million or 21.7 times. The change occurred at $257.2 million due to a 4.2-fold increase in prices, as also at $31.4 million due to a 1.6-fold increase in per capita rate, as well as at $33.1 million due to the expansion in population. The average annual growth in government expenditure is 4.9%. The minimum value of public expenditure was in 1971 at $5.8 million. The maximum value of government consumption expenditure was in 2019 at $427.3 million.

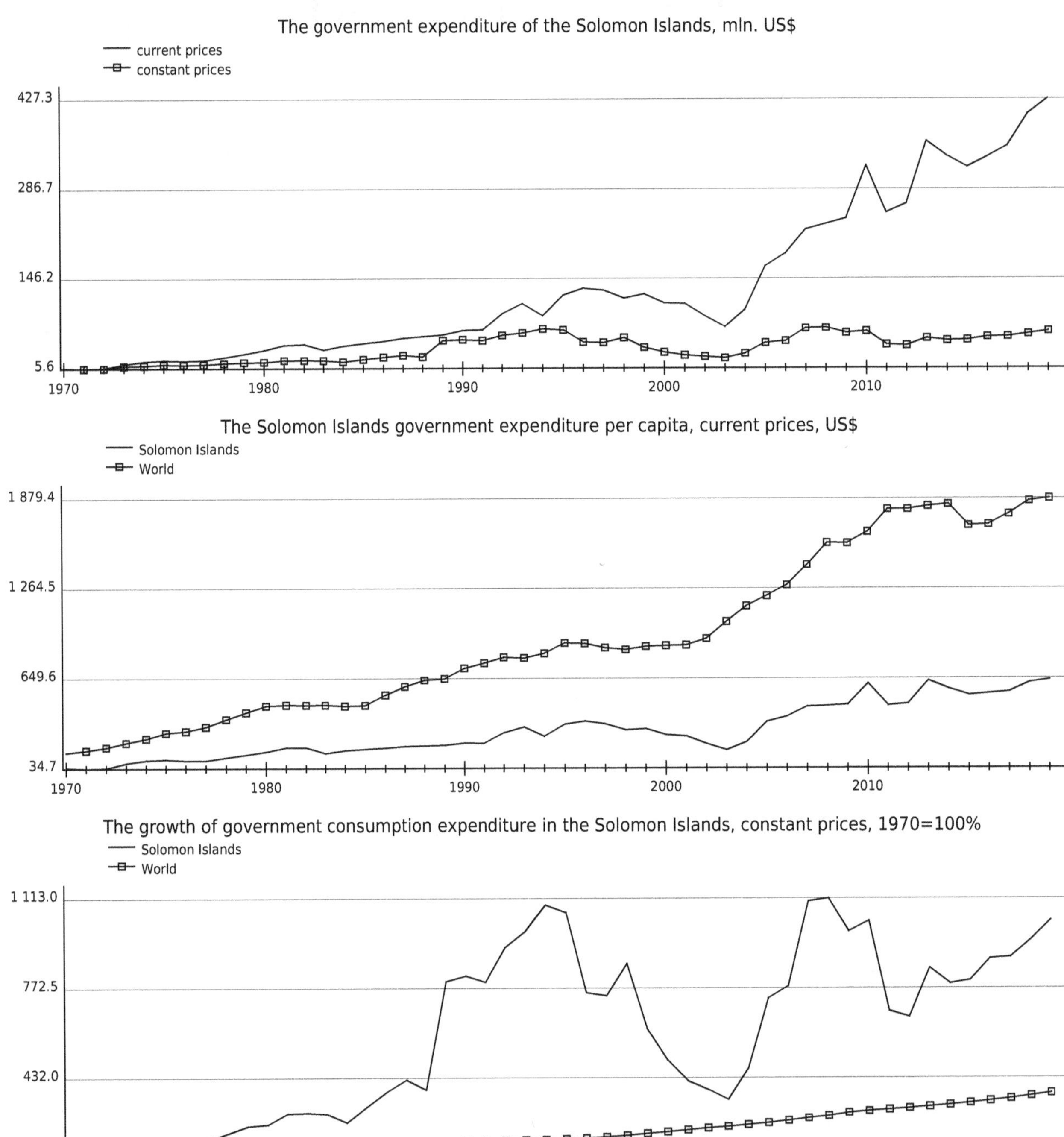

The government expenditure of the Solomon Islands, mln. US$

The Solomon Islands government expenditure per capita, current prices, US$

The growth of government consumption expenditure in the Solomon Islands, constant prices, 1970=100%

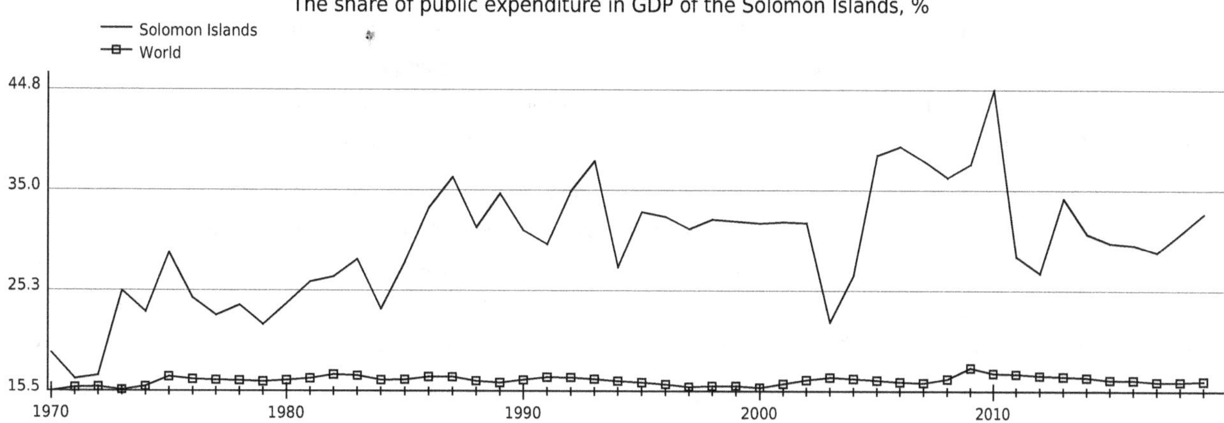

The share of public expenditure in GDP of the Solomon Islands, %

The 1970s

The Solomon Islands government expenditure was $15.5 million per year in the 1970s, ranked 162nd in the world, and was on a par with Laos ($15.8 million). The share in the world was 0.0014%, and 0.079% in Oceania.

The share of government consumption expenditure in GDP of the Solomon Islands was 23.0% in the 1970s, ranked 29th in the world, and was on a par with Greenland (23.0%).

The Solomon Islands public expenditure per capita was $81.5 in the 1970s, ranked 124th in the world, and was on a par with Egypt ($81.4), Saint Vincent and the Grenadines ($82.4). The public expenditure per capita in the Solomon Islands was less than government expenditure per capita in the world ($265.2) in 3.3 times, and was less than government expenditure per capita in Oceania ($920.9) in 11.3 times.

The growth of government expenditure in the Solomon Islands was 10.7% in the 1970s, ranked 19th in the world, and was on a par with the Turks and Caicos Islands (10.7%). The growth of government expenditure in the Solomon Islands (10.7%) was greater than growth of government expenditure in the world (3.7%), was greater than growth of government consumption expenditure in Oceania (3.9%).

Comparison with neighbors. The Solomon Islands public expenditure was greater than in Nauru ($6.0 million); but less than in Papua New Guinea ($653.5 million), in New Caledonia ($142.1 million), and in Vanuatu ($27.6 million). The Solomon Islands government expenditure per capita was less than in New Caledonia ($1 126.4), in Nauru ($845.4), in Vanuatu ($279.8), and in Papua New Guinea ($210.0). The growth of government expenditure in the Solomon Islands was greater than in Vanuatu (7.7%), in Papua New Guinea (0.14%), and in Nauru (-2.5%); but less than in New Caledonia (17.3%).

Comparison with leaders. The Solomon Islands public expenditure was less than in the United States ($285.9 billion), in the USSR ($117.3 billion), in Germany ($95.6 billion), in Japan ($78.0 billion), and in France ($64.5 billion). The government consumption expenditure per capita in the Solomon Islands was less than in the United States ($1 310.2), in Germany ($1 213.7), in France ($1 202.3), in Japan ($700.2), and in the USSR ($465.0). The growth of government consumption expenditure in the Solomon Islands was greater than in the USSR (7.2%), in Japan (5.3%), in France (5.0%), in Germany (4.4%), and in the USA (0.94%).

The 1980s

The public expenditure of the Solomon Islands was $45.6 million per year in the 1980s, ranked 160th in the world. The share in the world was 0.0018%, and 0.096% in Oceania.

The share of government consumption expenditure in GDP of the Solomon Islands was 29.2% in the 1980s, ranked 22nd in the world.

The government consumption expenditure per capita in the Solomon Islands was $170.9 in the 1980s, ranked 119th in the world, and was on a par with Asia ($170.1). The Solomon Islands government expenditure per capita was less than government consumption expenditure per capita in the world ($523.5) in 3.1 times, and was less than public expenditure per capita in Oceania ($1 914.7) in 11.2 times.

The growth of government consumption expenditure in the Solomon Islands was 12.3% in the 1980s, ranked 7th in the world, and was on a par with Macao (12.4%). The growth of government expenditure in the Solomon Islands (12.3%) was greater than growth of public expenditure in the world (2.7%), was greater than growth of public expenditure in Oceania (3.4%).

Comparison with neighbors. The Solomon Islands government consumption expenditure was greater than in Nauru ($16.7 million); but less than in Papua New Guinea ($1.1 billion), in New Caledonia ($413.7 million), and in Vanuatu ($48.0 million). The government consumption expenditure per capita in the Solomon Islands was less than in New Caledonia ($2.7 thousand), in Nauru ($1 972.9), in Vanuatu ($372.7), and in Papua New Guinea ($272.9). The growth of government expenditure in the Solomon Islands was greater than in Nauru (4.8%), in New Caledonia (4.7%), in Vanuatu (2.1%), and in Papua New Guinea (-0.71%).

Comparison with leaders. The Solomon Islands government consumption expenditure was less than in the USA ($665.3 billion), in Japan ($257.4 billion), in Germany ($203.7 billion), in the USSR ($181.1 billion), and in France ($159.8 billion). The government expenditure per capita in the Solomon Islands was less than in France ($2.8 thousand), in the United States ($2.8 thousand), in Germany ($2.6 thousand), in Japan ($2.1 thousand), and in the USSR ($658.0). The growth of government consumption expenditure in the Solomon Islands was greater than in the USSR (5.4%), in Japan (3.5%), in France (2.8%), in the USA (2.6%), and in Germany (0.98%).

The 1990s

The Solomon Islands public expenditure was $103.3 million per year in the 1990s, ranked 178th in the world, and was on a par with Antigua and Barbuda ($102.0 million), Somalia ($104.7 million). The share in the world was 0.0022%, and 0.13% in Oceania.

The share of government expenditure in GDP of the Solomon Islands was 32.2% in the 1990s, ranked 16th in the world, and was on a par with Lesotho (32.5%).

The public expenditure per capita in the Solomon Islands was $290.7 in the 1990s, ranked 115th in the world, and was on a par with Algeria ($288.1), Colombia ($294.5), Jordan ($297.4). The Solomon Islands government consumption expenditure per capita was less than public expenditure per capita in the world ($824.8) in 2.8 times, and was less than government expenditure per capita in Oceania ($2 816.0) in 9.7 times.

The growth of government consumption expenditure in the Solomon Islands was -2.5% in the 1990s, ranked 182nd in the world, and was on a par with Uzbekistan (-2.5%), Congo (-2.5%). The growth of public expenditure in the Solomon Islands (-2.5%) was less than growth of government consumption expenditure in the world (2.0%), was less than growth of government expenditure in Oceania (2.8%).

Comparison with neighbors. The government expenditure of the Solomon Islands was greater than in Vanuatu ($61.4 million) and in Nauru ($12.5 million); but less than in Papua New Guinea ($1.4 billion) and in New Caledonia ($940.3 million). The government expenditure per capita in the Solomon Islands was greater than in Papua New Guinea ($267.4); but less than in New Caledonia ($4.9 thousand), in Nauru ($1 209.6), and in Vanuatu ($371.8). The growth of government expenditure in the Solomon Islands was greater than in Vanuatu (-3.3%) and in Nauru (-14.0%); but less than in New Caledonia (2.3%) and in Papua New Guinea (0.25%).

Comparison with leaders. The Solomon Islands government expenditure was less than in the USA ($1.1 trillion), in Japan ($651.8 billion), in Germany ($419.6 billion), in France ($325.4 billion), and in the United Kingdom ($234.6 billion). The Solomon Islands government expenditure per capita was less than in France ($5.5 thousand), in Germany ($5.2 thousand), in Japan ($5.2 thousand), in the USA ($4.3 thousand), and in the UK ($4.1 thousand). The growth of public expenditure in the Solomon Islands was less than in Japan (3.0%), in Germany (2.4%), in the United Kingdom (2.1%), in France (1.8%), and in the USA (1.3%).

The 2000s

The government consumption expenditure of the Solomon Islands was $151.3 million per year in the 2000s, ranked 184th in the world. The share in the world was 0.0019%, and 0.10% in Oceania.

The share of government consumption expenditure in GDP of the Solomon Islands was 34.5% in the 2000s, ranked 14th in the world.

The Solomon Islands government consumption expenditure per capita was $326.1 in the 2000s, ranked 135th in the world, and was on a par with Ecuador ($329.2). The Solomon Islands government consumption expenditure per capita was less than government consumption expenditure per capita in the world ($1 200.9) in 3.7 times, and was less than government expenditure per capita in Oceania ($4 445.7) in 13.6 times.

The growth of government consumption expenditure in the Solomon Islands was 4.8% in the 2000s, ranked 75th in the world, and was on a par with Peru (4.8%), Serbia (4.8%). The growth of government consumption expenditure in the Solomon Islands (4.8%) was greater than growth of public expenditure in the world (3.1%), was greater than growth of government consumption expenditure in

Oceania (3.1%).

Comparison with neighbors. The Solomon Islands government consumption expenditure was greater than in Vanuatu ($60.8 million) and in Nauru ($10.7 million); but less than in New Caledonia ($1.6 billion) and in Papua New Guinea ($1.2 billion). The government consumption expenditure per capita in the Solomon Islands was greater than in Vanuatu ($293.7) and in Papua New Guinea ($192.6); but less than in New Caledonia ($6.7 thousand) and in Nauru ($1 066.6). The growth of government consumption expenditure in the Solomon Islands was greater than in New Caledonia (2.5%), in Vanuatu (1.3%), and in Nauru (0.43%); but less than in Papua New Guinea (5.5%).

Comparison with leaders. The government expenditure of the Solomon Islands was less than in the USA ($1.9 trillion), in Japan ($844.2 billion), in Germany ($520.1 billion), in France ($479.9 billion), and in the United Kingdom ($453.4 billion). The government expenditure per capita in the Solomon Islands was less than in France ($7.6 thousand), in the UK ($7.5 thousand), in Japan ($6.6 thousand), in the United States ($6.5 thousand), and in Germany ($6.4 thousand). The growth of government consumption expenditure in the Solomon Islands was greater than in the UK (2.9%), in the United States (2.2%), in Japan (1.7%), in France (1.7%), and in Germany (1.4%).

The 2010s

The government expenditure of the Solomon Islands was $337.3 million per year in the 2010s, ranked 179th in the world, and was on a par with San Marino ($337.9 million). The share in the world was 0.0026%, and 0.11% in Oceania.

The share of public expenditure in GDP of the Solomon Islands was 31.4% in the 2010s, ranked 15th in the world.

The public expenditure per capita in the Solomon Islands was $565.4 in the 2010s, ranked 140th in the world, and was on a par with Papua New Guinea ($559.2), Georgia ($555.2). The Solomon Islands government expenditure per capita was less than public expenditure per capita in the world ($1 785.1) in 3.2 times, and was less than public expenditure per capita in Oceania ($7 863.2) in 13.9 times.

The growth of public expenditure in the Solomon Islands was 0.4% in the 2010s, ranked 171st in the world. The growth of government consumption expenditure in the Solomon Islands (0.43%) was less than growth of government expenditure in the world (2.3%), was less than growth of public expenditure in Oceania (3.3%).

Comparison with neighbors. The government expenditure of the Solomon Islands was 2.6 times higher than in Vanuatu ($129.3 million) and 7.7 times higher than in Nauru ($43.8 million); but 13.3 times lower than in Papua New Guinea ($4.5 billion) and 6.9 times lower than in New Caledonia ($2.3 billion). The government expenditure per capita in the Solomon Islands was 1.1% higher than in Papua New Guinea ($559.2) and 17.0% higher than in Vanuatu ($483.1); but 15.2 times lower than in New Caledonia ($8.6 thousand) and 7.5 times lower than in Nauru ($4.2 thousand). The growth of government consumption expenditure in the Solomon Islands was greater than in Papua New Guinea (-9.4%); but less than in Nauru (10.8%), in Vanuatu (3.2%), and in New Caledonia (1.8%).

Comparison with leaders. The Solomon Islands public expenditure was 7 867.4 times lower than in the United States ($2.7 trillion), 4 978.7 times lower than in China ($1.7 trillion), 3 092.5 times lower than in Japan ($1.0 trillion), 2 139.5 times lower than in Germany ($721.6 billion), and 1 891.4 times lower than in France ($637.9 billion). The government consumption expenditure per capita in the Solomon Islands was 17.0 times lower than in France ($9.6 thousand), 15.6 times lower than in Germany ($8.8 thousand), 14.7 times lower than in the USA ($8.3 thousand), 14.4 times lower than in Japan ($8.2 thousand), and 2.1 times lower than in China ($1 197.3). The growth of government consumption expenditure in the Solomon Islands was greater than in the United States (0.0052%); but less than in China (8.3%), in Germany (1.9%), in Japan (1.3%), and in France (1.3%).

Chapter XIII. Household consumption expenditure

(including Non-profit institutions serving households)

The Solomon Islands household expenditure enlarged from $38.7 million per year in the 1970s to $636.5 million per year in the 2010s, that is by $597.8 million or 16.4 times. The change occurred at $473.0 million due to a 3.9-fold increase in prices, as also at $42.3 million due to a 1.3-fold increase in per capita rate, as well as at $82.5 million due to the growth in population. The average annual growth in household expenditure is 3.5%. The minimum value of household expenditure was in 1970 at $26.1 million. The maximum value of household consumption expenditure was in 2019 at $824.1 million.

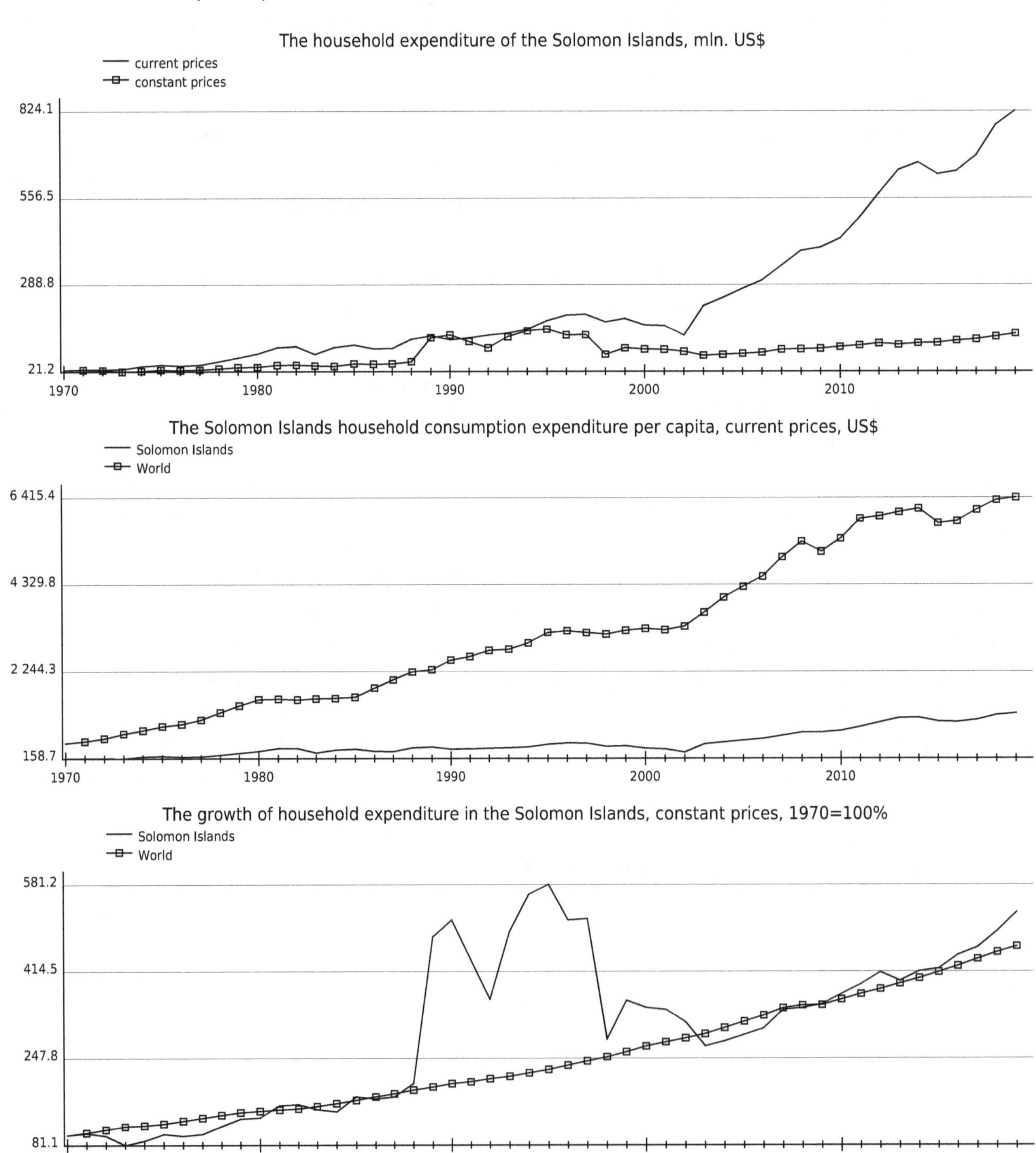

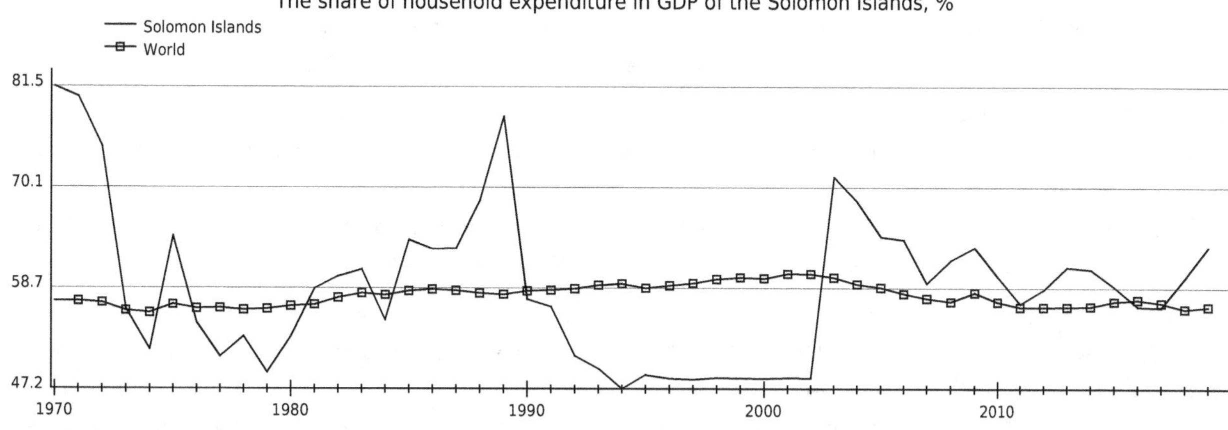

The 1970s

The Solomon Islands household expenditure was $38.7 million per year in the 1970s, ranked 165th in the world. The share in the world was 0.0010%, and 0.060% in Oceania.

The share of household expenditure in GDP of the Solomon Islands was 57.4% in the 1970s, ranked 126th in the world, and was on a par with Germany (57.4%), Middle Africa (57.7%), Ivory Coast (57.9%).

The Solomon Islands household expenditure per capita was $203.2 in the 1970s, ranked 147th in the world, and was on a par with Madagascar ($205.5), Sierra Leone ($199.0). The Solomon Islands household consumption expenditure per capita was less than household expenditure per capita in the world ($914.8) in 4.5 times, and was less than household consumption expenditure per capita in Oceania ($3 038.8) in 15.0 times.

The growth of household consumption expenditure in the Solomon Islands was 3.1% in the 1970s, ranked 135th in the world, and was on a par with Australasia (3.1%), Oceania (3.1%), Bermuda (3.1%). The growth of household consumption expenditure in the Solomon Islands (3.1%) was less than growth of household consumption expenditure in the world (4.1%), was greater than growth of household consumption expenditure in Oceania (3.1%).

Comparison with neighbors. The Solomon Islands household consumption expenditure was greater than in Nauru ($13.6 million); but less than in Papua New Guinea ($1.1 billion), in New Caledonia ($362.8 million), and in Vanuatu ($49.8 million). The household consumption expenditure per capita in the Solomon Islands was less than in New Caledonia ($2.9 thousand), in Nauru ($1 913.6), in Vanuatu ($504.7), and in Papua New Guinea ($368.4). The growth of household expenditure in the Solomon Islands was greater than in New Caledonia (2.4%), in Papua New Guinea (1.8%), and in Nauru (0.84%); but less than in Vanuatu (7.7%).

Comparison with leaders. The household consumption expenditure of the Solomon Islands was less than in the United States ($1.0 trillion), in the USSR ($310.6 billion), in Japan ($280.9 billion), in Germany ($277.8 billion), and in France ($180.7 billion). The Solomon Islands household expenditure per capita was less than in the United States ($4.7 thousand), in Germany ($3.5 thousand), in France ($3.4 thousand), in Japan ($2.5 thousand), and in the USSR ($1 231.6). The growth of household consumption expenditure in the Solomon Islands was less than in Japan (5.1%), in the USSR (4.7%), in France (4.0%), in the United States (3.6%), and in Germany (3.6%).

The 1980s

The household consumption expenditure of the Solomon Islands was $97.8 million per year in the 1980s, ranked 165th in the world, and was on a par with Tonga ($98.1 million), the Seychelles ($96.5 million), Dominica ($100.2 million). The share in the world was 0.0011%, and 0.068% in Oceania.

The share of household consumption expenditure in GDP of the Solomon Islands was 62.6% in the 1980s, ranked 98th in the world, and was on a par with Greenland (62.6%), the USA (62.6%), the Americas (62.3%).

The household expenditure per capita in the Solomon Islands was $366.5 in the 1980s, ranked 143rd in the world, and was on a par with Kenya ($369.7), Lesotho ($369.8), Mongolia ($361.3). The Solomon Islands household consumption expenditure per capita was less than household consumption expenditure per capita in the world ($1 808.0) in 4.9 times, and was less than household expenditure per capita in Oceania ($5 842.6) in 15.9 times.

The growth of household consumption expenditure in the Solomon Islands was 13.8% in the 1980s, ranked 1st in the world. The growth of household consumption expenditure in the Solomon Islands (13.8%) was greater than growth of household consumption expenditure in the world (3.0%), was greater than growth of household expenditure in Oceania (3.1%).

Comparison with neighbors. The household consumption expenditure of the Solomon Islands was greater than in Vanuatu ($91.5 million) and in Nauru ($43.3 million); but less than in Papua New Guinea ($2.5 billion) and in New Caledonia ($681.8 million). The household consumption expenditure per capita in the Solomon Islands was less than in Nauru ($5.1 thousand), in New Caledonia ($4.4 thousand), in Vanuatu ($710.9), and in Papua New Guinea ($615.2). The growth of household expenditure in the Solomon Islands was greater than in Nauru (4.6%), in New Caledonia (3.9%), in Vanuatu (3.8%), and in Papua New Guinea (0.90%).

Comparison with leaders. The household expenditure of the Solomon Islands was less than in the USA ($2.6 trillion), in Japan ($945.6 billion), in Germany ($575.7 billion), in the USSR ($424.6 billion), and in the United Kingdom ($416.5 billion). The Solomon Islands household expenditure per capita was less than in the United States ($10.9 thousand), in Japan ($7.8 thousand), in Germany ($7.4 thousand), in the United Kingdom ($7.4 thousand), and in the USSR ($1 542.8). The growth of household expenditure in the Solomon Islands was greater than in Japan (3.7%), in the UK (3.5%), in the USA (3.2%), in the USSR (3.0%), and in Germany (1.8%).

The 1990s

The household consumption expenditure of the Solomon Islands was $159.8 million per year in the 1990s, ranked 192nd in the world, and was on a par with Samoa ($157.3 million). The share in the world was 0.0009%, and 0.062% in Oceania.

The share of household consumption expenditure in GDP of the Solomon Islands was 49.8% in the 1990s, ranked 179th in the world, and was on a par with Czechia (49.8%), the Netherlands (49.8%), Papua New Guinea (49.7%).

The Solomon Islands household expenditure per capita was $449.7 in the 1990s, ranked 159th in the world, and was on a par with Mongolia ($453.2), Armenia ($443.3). The household consumption expenditure per capita in the Solomon Islands was less than household consumption expenditure per capita in the world ($2 963.9) in 6.6 times, and was less than household expenditure per capita in Oceania ($8 928.2) in 19.9 times.

The growth of household consumption expenditure in the Solomon Islands was -2.9% in the 1990s, ranked 186th in the world, and was on a par with Cuba (-2.9%). The growth of household consumption expenditure in the Solomon Islands (-2.9%) was less than growth of household expenditure in the world (3.0%), was less than growth of household expenditure in Oceania (3.2%).

Comparison with neighbors. The Solomon Islands household consumption expenditure was greater than in Vanuatu ($151.4 million) and in Nauru ($32.4 million); but less than in Papua New Guinea ($3.3 billion) and in New Caledonia ($2.1 billion). The household consumption expenditure per capita in the Solomon Islands was less than in New Caledonia ($11.0 thousand), in Nauru ($3.1 thousand), in Vanuatu ($917.4), and in Papua New Guinea ($642.2). The growth of household expenditure in the Solomon Islands was greater than in Nauru (-14.0%); but less than in Papua New Guinea (7.1%), in New Caledonia (5.1%), and in Vanuatu (4.1%).

Comparison with leaders. The Solomon Islands household expenditure was less than in the United States ($4.9 trillion), in Japan ($2.3 trillion), in Germany ($1.2 trillion), in the UK ($884.5 billion), and in France ($783.0 billion). The Solomon Islands household consumption expenditure per capita was less than in the United States ($18.5 thousand), in Japan ($18.2 thousand), in the UK ($15.3 thousand), in Germany ($15.2 thousand), and in France ($13.2 thousand). The growth of household consumption expenditure in the Solomon Islands was less than in the United States (3.4%), in the United Kingdom (2.8%), in Germany (2.1%), in Japan (1.8%), and in France (1.8%).

The 2000s

The household consumption expenditure of the Solomon Islands was $265.7 million per year in the 2000s, ranked 196th in the world. The share in the world was 0.0010%, and 0.056% in Oceania.

The share of household expenditure in GDP of the Solomon Islands was 60.5% in the 2000s, ranked 129th in the world, and was on a par with Latvia (60.5%), Ukraine (60.6%), Southern Africa (60.7%).

The household consumption expenditure per capita in the Solomon Islands was $572.6 in the 2000s, ranked 169th in the world, and was on a par with Papua New Guinea ($573.1), Pakistan ($566.6), Zimbabwe ($562.8). The Solomon Islands household consumption expenditure per capita was less than household expenditure per capita in the world ($4 208.2) in 7.3 times, and was less than household consumption expenditure per capita in Oceania ($14 250.8) in 24.9 times.

The growth of household consumption expenditure in the Solomon Islands was -0.2% in the 2000s, ranked 202nd in the world. The growth of household expenditure in the Solomon Islands (-0.21%) was less than growth of household consumption expenditure in the world (3.0%), was less than growth of household expenditure in Oceania (3.6%).

Comparison with neighbors. The Solomon Islands household consumption expenditure was greater than in Vanuatu ($256.7 million) and in Nauru ($27.7 million); but less than in New Caledonia ($3.9 billion) and in Papua New Guinea ($3.7 billion). The household expenditure per capita in the Solomon Islands was less than in New Caledonia ($16.5 thousand), in Nauru ($2.8 thousand), in Vanuatu ($1 240.3), and in Papua New Guinea ($573.1). The growth of household expenditure in the Solomon Islands was less than in New Caledonia (2.6%), in Vanuatu (2.3%), in Papua New Guinea (2.1%), and in Nauru (0.43%).

Comparison with leaders. The household consumption expenditure of the Solomon Islands was less than in the USA ($8.5 trillion), in Japan ($2.6 trillion), in Germany ($1.5 trillion), in the United Kingdom ($1.5 trillion), and in France ($1.1 trillion). The household expenditure per capita in the Solomon Islands was less than in the USA ($28.8 thousand), in the UK ($25.0 thousand), in Japan ($20.4 thousand), in Germany ($18.9 thousand), and in France ($18.1 thousand). The growth of household consumption expenditure in the Solomon Islands was less than in the USA (2.4%), in the United Kingdom (2.1%), in France (2.0%), in Japan (0.81%), and in Germany (0.46%).

The 2010s

The Solomon Islands household consumption expenditure was $636.5 million per year in the 2010s, ranked 193rd in the world, and was on a par with Saint Kitts and Nevis ($629.5 million), San Marino ($649.0 million). The share in the world was 0.0014%, and 0.067% in Oceania.

The share of household consumption expenditure in GDP of the Solomon Islands was 59.3% in the 2010s, ranked 134th in the world, and was on a par with Southern Asia (59.4%), Uzbekistan (58.9%), Poland (59.7%).

The household expenditure per capita in the Solomon Islands was $1 067.1 in the 2010s, ranked 166th in the world, and was on a par with Southern Asia ($1 069.7), Kyrgyzstan ($1 043.0). The Solomon Islands household expenditure per capita was less than household expenditure per capita in the world ($6 018.5) in 5.6 times, and was less than household consumption expenditure per capita in Oceania ($24 058.7) in 22.5 times.

The growth of household expenditure in the Solomon Islands was 4.1% in the 2010s, ranked 70th in the world, and was on a par with Monaco (4.1%), Cuba (4.1%), Morocco (4.2%). The growth of household expenditure in the Solomon Islands (4.1%) was greater than growth of household consumption expenditure in the world (2.8%), was greater than growth of household consumption expenditure in Oceania (2.3%).

Comparison with neighbors. The Solomon Islands household expenditure was 24.8% higher than in Vanuatu ($509.9 million) and 5.6 times higher than in Nauru ($114.0 million); but 19.9 times lower than in Papua New Guinea ($12.7 billion) and 9.7 times lower than in New Caledonia ($6.2 billion). The Solomon Islands household expenditure per capita was 21.5 times lower than in New Caledonia ($23.0 thousand), 10.3 times lower than in Nauru ($11.0 thousand), 44.0% lower than in Vanuatu ($1 905.2), and 32.4% lower than in Papua New Guinea ($1 579.5). The growth of household consumption expenditure in the Solomon Islands was greater than in New Caledonia (2.9%) and in Vanuatu (2.7%); but less than in Papua New Guinea (12.3%) and in Nauru (10.8%).

Comparison with leaders. The household consumption expenditure of the Solomon Islands was 19 153.7 times lower than in the United States ($12.2 trillion), 6 173.2 times lower than in China ($3.9 trillion), 4 693.2 times lower than in Japan ($3.0 trillion), 3 076.7 times lower than in Germany ($2.0 trillion), and 2 799.4 times lower than in the United Kingdom ($1.8 trillion). The Solomon Islands household consumption expenditure per capita was 35.8 times lower than in the United States ($38.2 thousand), 25.5 times lower than in the UK ($27.2 thousand), 22.4 times lower than in Germany ($23.9 thousand), 21.9 times lower than in Japan ($23.4 thousand), and 2.6 times lower than in China ($2.8 thousand). The growth of household consumption expenditure in the Solomon Islands was greater than in the USA (2.4%), in the UK (1.8%), in Germany (1.4%), and in Japan (0.64%); but less than in China (8.3%).

Chapter XIV. Food consumption

During the research period the food consumption grew in stimulants (in 5.6 times), cereals (in 2.1 times), alcoholic beverages (by 78.2%), pulses (by 41.9%), vegetable oils (by 20.8%), spices (by 9.6%), fruits (by 7.3%), eggs (by 7.1%), but fell in sugar (by 1.3%), meat (by 12.8%), starchy roots (by 22.2%), milk (by 48.4%), vegetables (by 60.4%), fish (by 67.7%), treenuts (by 94.4%).

These are the correlation coefficients between the GNI per capita in constant prices and the food consumption: pulses (0.957), stimulants (0.95), cereals (0.913), alcoholic beverages (0.558), fruits (0.368), vegetable oils (0.363), eggs (0.342), spices (0.337), sugar (-0.281), meat (-0.339), milk (-0.644), starchy roots (-0.739), treenuts (-0.859), fish (-0.86), vegetables (-0.972).

The 1970s

Kcal supply in the Solomon Islands was 2 211.7 kcal/capita/day in the 1970s, ranked 92nd in the world, and was on a par with Ecuador (2 213.1 kcal/capita/day), Sri Lanka (2 214.4 kcal/capita/day), Panama (2 220.7 kcal/capita/day). Kcal supply in the Solomon Islands was less than in the world (2 403.2 kcal/capita/day), and was less than in Oceania (3 054.0 kcal/capita/day). Structure of kcal supply: starchy roots (46.8%), cereals (17.3%), meat (5.1%), fish (4.9%), sugar (3.4%), and others (22.5%).

Protein supply in the Solomon Islands was 55.7 g/capita/day in the 1970s, ranked 97th in the world, and was on a par with Yemen (56.0 g/capita/day), Suriname (56.2 g/capita/day), Sudan (56.2 g/capita/day). Protein supply in the Solomon Islands was less than in the world (65.0 g/capita/day), and was less than in Oceania (103.8 g/capita/day). Structure of protein supply: fish (30.1%), starchy roots (26%), cereals (14.8%), meat (10.2%), pulses (7.2%), and others (11.7%).

Fat supply in the Solomon Islands was 49.7 g/capita/day in the 1970s, ranked 84th in the world, and was on a par with the Dominican Republic (49.7 g/capita/day). Fat supply in the Solomon Islands was less than in the world (55.1 g/capita/day), and was less than in Oceania (112.0 g/capita/day). Structure of fat supply: meat (19.6%), vegetable oils (15.5%), fish (8.2%), starchy roots (5.8%), cereals (2.4%), and others (48.5%).

These are the levels of food consumption in the world rankings: 2nd - starchy roots (405.7 kg/capita/yr), 5th - fish (58.2 kg/capita/yr), 47th - treenuts (0.97 kg/capita/yr), 49th - pulses (6.7 kg/capita/yr), 60th - spices (0.42 kg/capita/yr), 84th - fruits (50.5 kg/capita/yr), 98th - meat (15.4 kg/capita/yr), 103rd - eggs (1.3 kg/capita/yr), 109th - vegetables (23.1 kg/capita/yr), 113th - alcoholic beverages (6.2 kg/capita/yr), 118th - vegetable oils (2.8 kg/capita/yr), 120th - milk (14.4 kg/capita/yr), 121st - stimulants (0.28 kg/capita/yr), 123rd - sugar (8.2 kg/capita/yr), 144th - cereals (44.5 kg/capita/yr).

The 1980s

Kcal supply in the Solomon Islands was 2 218.5 kcal/capita/day in the 1980s, ranked 105th in the world, and was on a par with Rwanda (2 211.3 kcal/capita/day), Pakistan (2 230.6 kcal/capita/day), El Salvador (2 232.9 kcal/capita/day). Kcal supply in the Solomon Islands was less than in the world (2 572.3 kcal/capita/day), and was less than in Oceania (3 045.2 kcal/capita/day). Structure of kcal supply: starchy roots (39.9%), cereals (23.6%), fish (4.9%), meat (4.7%), sugar (3.9%), and others (23%).

Protein supply in the Solomon Islands was 56.1 g/capita/day in the 1980s, ranked 103rd in the world, and was on a par with Tanzania (56.0 g/capita/day), Madagascar (56.0 g/capita/day), Saint Vincent (56.6 g/capita/day). Protein supply in the Solomon Islands was less than in the world (69.1 g/capita/day), and was less than in Oceania (101.6 g/capita/day). Structure of protein supply: fish (28.9%), starchy roots (22.7%), cereals (19.9%), meat (10.2%), pulses (7.2%), and others (11.1%).

Fat supply in the Solomon Islands was 50.7 g/capita/day in the 1980s, ranked 92nd in the world, and was on a par with Pakistan (50.4 g/capita/day). Fat supply in the Solomon Islands was less than in the world (63.2 g/capita/day), and was less than in Oceania (116.3 g/capita/day). Structure of fat supply: vegetable oils (19%), meat (17.6%), fish (8.2%), starchy roots (4.9%), cereals (3.2%), and others (47.1%).

These are the levels of food consumption in the world rankings: 1st - starchy roots (350.1 kg/capita/yr), 5th - fish (52.9 kg/capita/yr), 48th - pulses (6.7 kg/capita/yr), 60th - treenuts (0.70 kg/capita/yr), 65th - spices (0.42 kg/capita/yr), 102nd - fruits (46.3 kg/capita/yr), 105th - meat (14.9 kg/capita/yr), 109th - alcoholic beverages (8.8 kg/capita/yr), 118th - eggs (1.0 kg/capita/yr), 120th - sugar (9.3 kg/capita/yr), 124th - vegetables (21.2 kg/capita/yr), 127th - milk (14.5 kg/capita/yr), 142nd - cereals (60.2 kg/capita/yr).

The 1990s

Kcal supply in the Solomon Islands was 2 270.5 kcal/capita/day in the 1990s, ranked 118th in the world, and was on a par with Panama

(2 267.9 kcal/capita/day), Guinea-Bissau (2 267.2 kcal/capita/day), Guatemala (2 259.9 kcal/capita/day). Kcal supply in the Solomon Islands was less than in the world (2 652.6 kcal/capita/day), and was less than in Oceania (3 065.5 kcal/capita/day). Structure of kcal supply: starchy roots (36.6%), cereals (30.3%), fish (4.2%), sugar (3.5%), meat (3.4%), and others (22%).

Protein supply in the Solomon Islands was 52.8 g/capita/day in the 1990s, ranked 136th in the world, and was on a par with Indonesia (52.7 g/capita/day), Bolivia (53.3 g/capita/day), Ivory Coast (53.3 g/capita/day). Protein supply in the Solomon Islands was less than in the world (72.1 g/capita/day), and was less than in Oceania (100.9 g/capita/day). Structure of protein supply: fish (26.7%), cereals (25.3%), starchy roots (22.6%), pulses (8.4%), meat (6.4%), and others (10.6%).

Fat supply in the Solomon Islands was 48.1 g/capita/day in the 1990s, ranked 126th in the world, and was on a par with Bosnia and Herzegovina (48.1 g/capita/day), Congo (47.9 g/capita/day), Burkina Faso (48.3 g/capita/day). Fat supply in the Solomon Islands was less than in the world (69.0 g/capita/day), and was less than in Oceania (124.1 g/capita/day). Structure of fat supply: vegetable oils (15.8%), meat (14.5%), fish (8.1%), starchy roots (4.9%), cereals (3.6%), and others (53.1%).

These are the levels of food consumption in the world rankings: 2nd - starchy roots (328.1 kg/capita/yr), 14th - fish (42.5 kg/capita/yr), 43rd - pulses (7.3 kg/capita/yr), 86th - spices (0.36 kg/capita/yr), 92nd - treenuts (0.65 kg/capita/yr), 119th - fruits (40.9 kg/capita/yr), 129th - stimulants (0.71 kg/capita/yr), 142nd - alcoholic beverages (4.2 kg/capita/yr), 146th - eggs (0.94 kg/capita/yr), 153rd - meat (9.7 kg/capita/yr), 154th - milk (9.9 kg/capita/yr), 155th - vegetable oils (2.8 kg/capita/yr), 159th - cereals (74.5 kg/capita/yr), 160th - vegetables (17.5 kg/capita/yr).

The 2000s

Kcal supply in the Solomon Islands was 2 410.9 kcal/capita/day in the 2000s, ranked 123rd in the world, and was on a par with Niger (2 422.2 kcal/capita/day), Peru (2 398.8 kcal/capita/day), Benin (2 431.7 kcal/capita/day). Kcal supply in the Solomon Islands was less than in the world (2 765.9 kcal/capita/day), and was less than in Oceania (3 090.9 kcal/capita/day). Structure of kcal supply: starchy roots (35.5%), cereals (32.9%), sugar (3.8%), vegetable oils (3.4%), pulses (3.2%), and others (21.2%).

Protein supply in the Solomon Islands was 53.2 g/capita/day in the 2000s, ranked 155th in the world, and was on a par with Eastern Africa (53.0 g/capita/day). Protein supply in the Solomon Islands was less than in the world (76.5 g/capita/day), and was less than in Oceania (100.0 g/capita/day). Structure of protein supply: cereals (29.7%), starchy roots (23.4%), fish (20.2%), pulses (9.4%), meat (6.4%), and others (10.9%).

Fat supply in the Solomon Islands was 47.4 g/capita/day in the 2000s, ranked 149th in the world, and was on a par with Togo (47.4 g/capita/day), India (47.5 g/capita/day). Fat supply in the Solomon Islands was less than in the world (76.9 g/capita/day), and was less than in Oceania (130.3 g/capita/day). Structure of fat supply: vegetable oils (19.3%), meat (13.2%), fish (6.1%), starchy roots (5.1%), cereals (4.5%), and others (51.8%).

These are the levels of food consumption in the world rankings: 2nd - starchy roots (339.8 kg/capita/yr), 24th - fish (33.4 kg/capita/yr), 41st - pulses (8.3 kg/capita/yr), 88th - spices (0.49 kg/capita/yr), 117th - treenuts (0.54 kg/capita/yr), 128th - stimulants (1.2 kg/capita/yr), 131st - alcoholic beverages (8.6 kg/capita/yr), 146th - eggs (1.1 kg/capita/yr), 150th - sugar (9.3 kg/capita/yr), 156th - cereals (87.5 kg/capita/yr), 159th - meat (9.7 kg/capita/yr), 162nd - vegetable oils (3.4 kg/capita/yr), 165th - milk (6.4 kg/capita/yr), 167th - vegetables (17.4 kg/capita/yr).

The 2010s

Kcal supply in the Solomon Islands was 2 446.3 kcal/capita/day in the 2010s, ranked 134th in the world, and was on a par with India (2 447.8 kcal/capita/day), Senegal (2 440.5 kcal/capita/day), Bangladesh (2 438.3 kcal/capita/day). Kcal supply in the Solomon Islands was less than in the world (2 869.3 kcal/capita/day), and was less than in Oceania (3 193.3 kcal/capita/day). Structure of kcal supply: starchy roots (34.3%), cereals (33.8%), pulses (3.6%), vegetable oils (3.4%), meat (3.4%), and others (21.5%).

Protein supply in the Solomon Islands was 56.5 g/capita/day in the 2010s, ranked 156th in the world, and was on a par with Rwanda (56.7 g/capita/day), Tanzania (56.4 g/capita/day), Eastern Africa (57.0 g/capita/day). Protein supply in the Solomon Islands was less than in the world (80.6 g/capita/day), and was less than in Oceania (100.9 g/capita/day). Structure of protein supply: cereals (29.6%), starchy roots (21.6%), fish (18.9%), pulses (10.1%), meat (9.1%), and others (10.7%).

Fat supply in the Solomon Islands was 48.5 g/capita/day in the 2010s, ranked 152nd in the world, and was on a par with Kenya (48.7 g/capita/day), Uganda (48.1 g/capita/day), Chad (48.0 g/capita/day). Fat supply in the Solomon Islands was less than in the world

(82.4 g/capita/day), and was less than in Oceania (140.2 g/capita/day). Structure of fat supply: vegetable oils (19.2%), meat (14.2%), fish (5.7%), cereals (5.2%), starchy roots (4.8%), and others (50.9%).

These are the levels of food consumption in the world rankings: 2nd - starchy roots (331.9 kg/capita/yr), 24th - fish (34.7 kg/capita/yr), 44th - pulses (9.5 kg/capita/yr), 96th - spices (0.46 kg/capita/yr), 125th - treenuts (0.50 kg/capita/yr), 127th - fruits (54.2 kg/capita/yr), 129th - stimulants (1.6 kg/capita/yr), 133rd - alcoholic beverages (11.1 kg/capita/yr), 147th - eggs (1.4 kg/capita/yr), 154th - meat (13.6 kg/capita/yr), 159th - milk (9.7 kg/capita/yr), 161st - sugar (8.1 kg/capita/yr), 162nd - vegetable oils (3.4 kg/capita/yr), 171st - vegetables (14.4 kg/capita/yr).

Part V. Reproduction

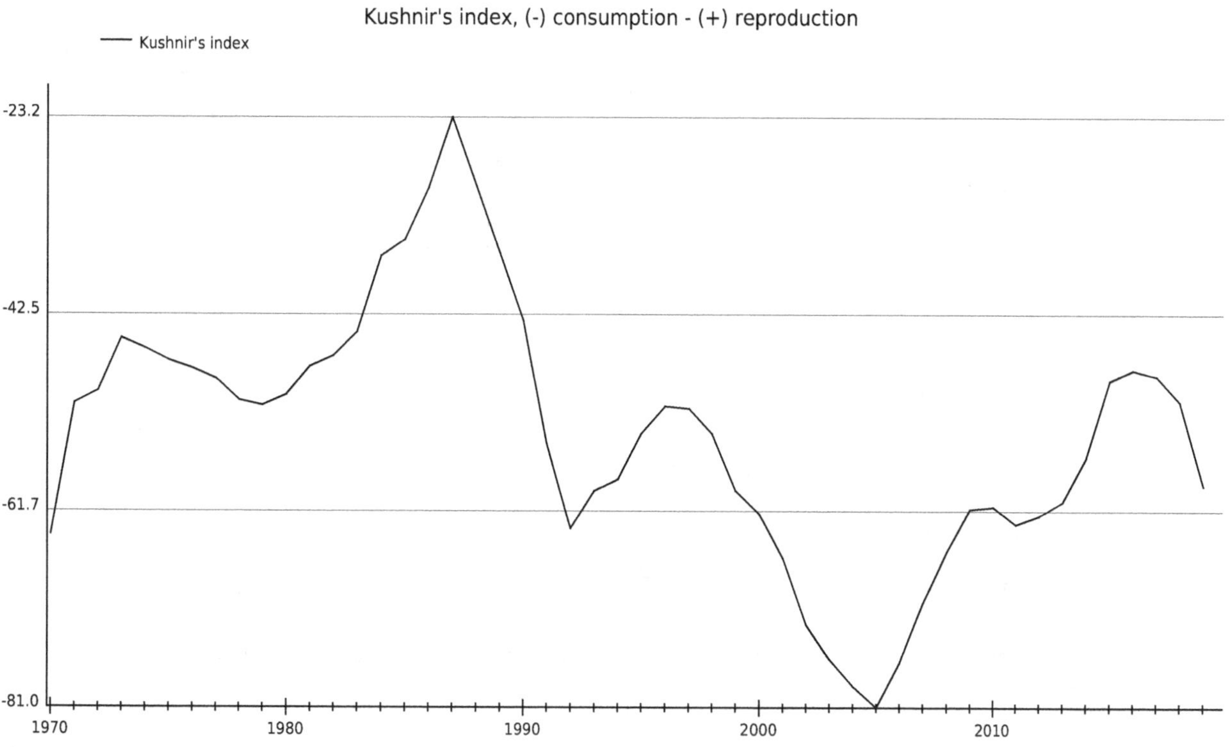

Chapter XV. Gross fixed capital formation

(including Acquisitions less disposals of valuables)

The Solomon Islands gross fixed capital formation grew up from $14.8 million per year in the 1970s to $162.3 million per year in the 2010s, that is by $147.6 million or 11.0 times. The change occurred at $125.0 million due to a 4.3-fold increase in prices, as also at -$8.9 million due to a 1.2-fold decrease in per capita rate, as well as at $31.5 million due to the increase in population. The average annual growth in fixed capital formation is 2.9%. The minimum value of fixed capital formation was in 1970 at $4.7 million. The maximum value of gross fixed capital formation was in 2017 at $206.4 million.

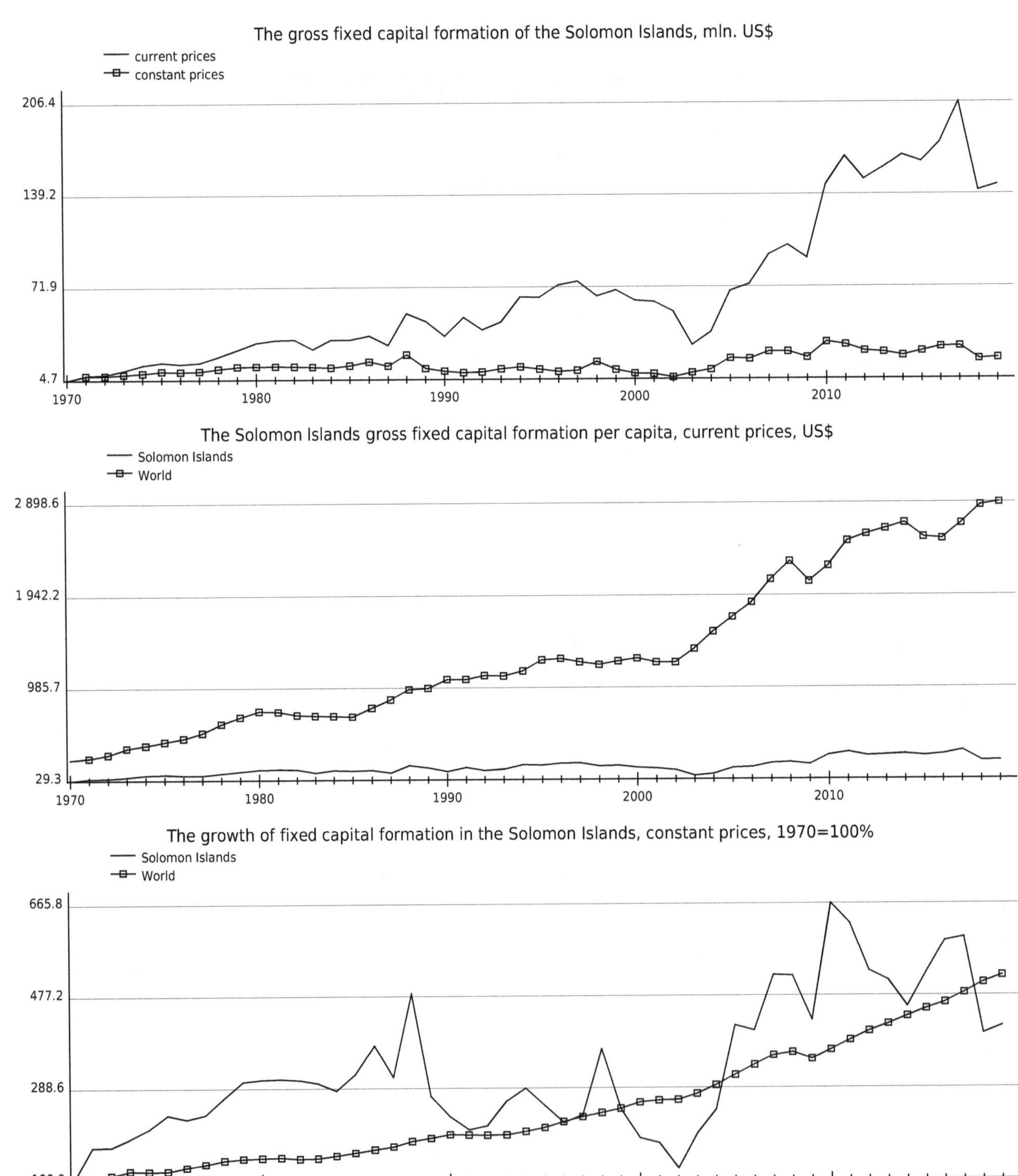

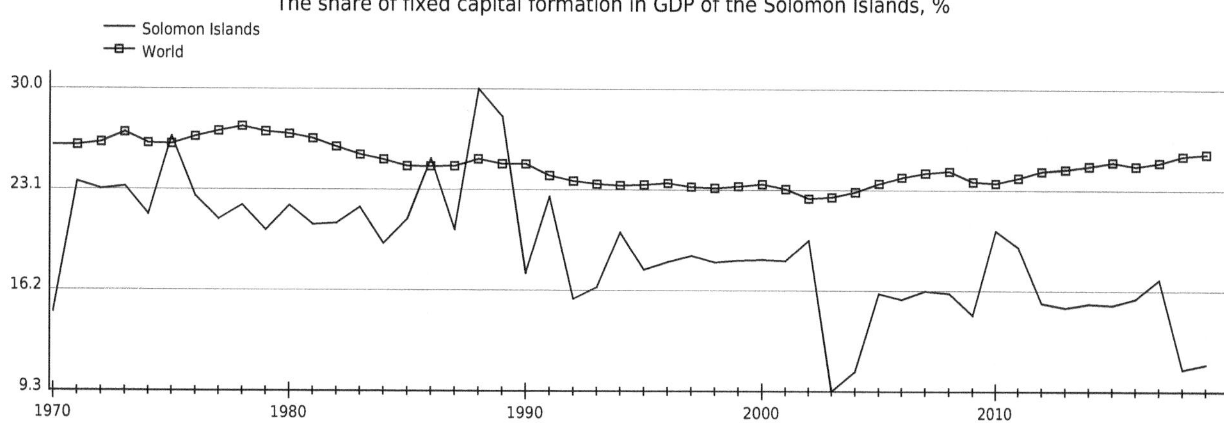

The 1970s

The Solomon Islands gross fixed capital formation was $14.8 million per year in the 1970s, ranked 163rd in the world, and was on a par with Laos ($14.9 million). The share in the world was 0.0008%, and 0.048% in Oceania.

The share of gross fixed capital formation in GDP of the Solomon Islands was 21.9% in the 1970s, ranked 106th in the world, and was on a par with Argentina (21.8%), Brazil (22.0%), Saudi Arabia (22.1%).

The gross fixed capital formation per capita in the Solomon Islands was $77.6 in the 1970s, ranked 140th in the world, and was on a par with Bolivia ($79.4). The fixed capital formation per capita in the Solomon Islands was less than fixed capital formation per capita in the world ($433.5) in 5.6 times, and was less than gross fixed capital formation per capita in Oceania ($1 437.8) in 18.5 times.

The growth of fixed capital formation in the Solomon Islands was 13.1% in the 1970s, ranked 28th in the world, and was on a par with Haiti (13.0%). The growth of fixed capital formation in the Solomon Islands (13.1%) was greater than growth of fixed capital formation in the world (4.2%), was greater than growth of fixed capital formation in Oceania (2.6%).

Comparison with neighbors. The Solomon Islands fixed capital formation was greater than in Nauru ($3.4 million); but less than in Papua New Guinea ($416.9 million), in New Caledonia ($196.2 million), and in Vanuatu ($17.4 million). The Solomon Islands fixed capital formation per capita was less than in New Caledonia ($1 555.8), in Nauru ($475.4), in Vanuatu ($176.5), and in Papua New Guinea ($134.0). The growth of fixed capital formation in the Solomon Islands was greater than in Nauru (11.5%), in Vanuatu (7.7%), in New Caledonia (-5.9%), and in Papua New Guinea (-7.9%).

Comparison with leaders. The Solomon Islands fixed capital formation was less than in the USA ($381.9 billion), in the USSR ($214.6 billion), in Japan ($191.6 billion), in Germany ($125.8 billion), and in France ($82.9 billion). The gross fixed capital formation per capita in the Solomon Islands was less than in the United States ($1 750.0), in Japan ($1 720.7), in Germany ($1 597.2), in France ($1 545.4), and in the USSR ($850.9). The growth of gross fixed capital formation in the Solomon Islands was greater than in the United States (4.4%), in Japan (3.9%), in the USSR (3.2%), in France (2.7%), and in Germany (1.5%).

The 1980s

The gross fixed capital formation of the Solomon Islands was $35.9 million per year in the 1980s, ranked 165th in the world. The share in the world was 0.0009%, and 0.051% in Oceania.

The share of gross fixed capital formation in GDP of the Solomon Islands was 23.0% in the 1980s, ranked 75th in the world, and was on a par with Eswatini (23.1%), the USA (23.0%), Southern Europe (23.1%).

The Solomon Islands gross fixed capital formation per capita was $134.8 in the 1980s, ranked 137th in the world, and was on a par with Nicaragua ($135.6), Indonesia ($132.5), Egypt ($131.5). The Solomon Islands fixed capital formation per capita was less than gross fixed capital formation per capita in the world ($790.9) in 5.9 times, and was less than gross fixed capital formation per capita in Oceania ($2 826.6) in 21.0 times.

The growth of fixed capital formation in the Solomon Islands was -1.1% in the 1980s, ranked 142nd in the world. The growth of gross fixed capital formation in the Solomon Islands (-1.1%) was less than growth of fixed capital formation in the world (2.5%), was less than growth of fixed capital formation in Oceania (4.9%).

Comparison with neighbors. The Solomon Islands gross fixed capital formation was greater than in Vanuatu ($29.0 million) and in Nauru ($18.8 million); but less than in Papua New Guinea ($955.0 million) and in New Caledonia ($251.9 million). The Solomon Islands fixed capital formation per capita was less than in Nauru ($2.2 thousand), in New Caledonia ($1 621.6), in Papua New Guinea ($236.9), and in Vanuatu ($225.3). The growth of gross fixed capital formation in the Solomon Islands was less than in Nauru (5.6%), in Vanuatu (3.6%), in New Caledonia (3.3%), and in Papua New Guinea (2.6%).

Comparison with leaders. The Solomon Islands gross fixed capital formation was less than in the USA ($958.4 billion), in Japan ($571.7 billion), in the USSR ($271.0 billion), in Germany ($238.1 billion), and in France ($164.3 billion). The fixed capital formation per capita in the Solomon Islands was less than in Japan ($4.7 thousand), in the United States ($4.0 thousand), in Germany ($3.1 thousand), in France ($2.9 thousand), and in the USSR ($984.8). The growth of fixed capital formation in the Solomon Islands was less than in Japan (4.8%), in the USA (3.1%), in France (2.4%), in the USSR (1.7%), and in Germany (1.4%).

The 1990s

The Solomon Islands gross fixed capital formation was $58.5 million per year in the 1990s, ranked 193rd in the world, and was on a par with Dominica ($57.2 million). The share in the world was 0.0009%, and 0.055% in Oceania.

The share of fixed capital formation in GDP of the Solomon Islands was 18.3% in the 1990s, ranked 156th in the world, and was on a par with Panama (18.2%), Samoa (18.2%), the Comoros (18.4%).

The Solomon Islands fixed capital formation per capita was $164.7 in the 1990s, ranked 157th in the world, and was on a par with Nicaragua ($166.6), Western Africa ($167.7), Djibouti ($168.4). The Solomon Islands gross fixed capital formation per capita was less than fixed capital formation per capita in the world ($1 183.8) in 7.2 times, and was less than gross fixed capital formation per capita in Oceania ($3 689.1) in 22.4 times.

The growth of gross fixed capital formation in the Solomon Islands was -1% in the 1990s, ranked 164th in the world, and was on a par with Slovakia (-1.0%). The growth of gross fixed capital formation in the Solomon Islands (-1.0%) was less than growth of fixed capital formation in the world (2.8%), was less than growth of gross fixed capital formation in Oceania (3.9%).

Comparison with neighbors. The gross fixed capital formation of the Solomon Islands was greater than in Vanuatu ($54.4 million) and in Nauru ($14.0 million); but less than in Papua New Guinea ($1.2 billion) and in New Caledonia ($704.6 million). The fixed capital formation per capita in the Solomon Islands was less than in New Caledonia ($3.7 thousand), in Nauru ($1 356.7), in Vanuatu ($329.3), and in Papua New Guinea ($239.2). The growth of gross fixed capital formation in the Solomon Islands was greater than in Nauru (-14.0%); but less than in Vanuatu (6.3%), in New Caledonia (2.8%), and in Papua New Guinea (0.31%).

Comparison with leaders. The gross fixed capital formation of the Solomon Islands was less than in the United States ($1.6 trillion), in Japan ($1.3 trillion), in Germany ($520.7 billion), in France ($299.3 billion), and in the United Kingdom ($250.0 billion). The Solomon Islands fixed capital formation per capita was less than in Japan ($10.4 thousand), in Germany ($6.5 thousand), in the United States ($6.1 thousand), in France ($5.0 thousand), and in the UK ($4.3 thousand). The growth of gross fixed capital formation in the Solomon Islands was less than in the United States (4.8%), in Germany (2.4%), in the United Kingdom (1.7%), in France (1.5%), and in Japan (0.18%).

The 2000s

The gross fixed capital formation of the Solomon Islands was $67.7 million per year in the 2000s, ranked 199th in the world. The share in the world was 0.0006%, and 0.031% in Oceania.

The share of fixed capital formation in GDP of the Solomon Islands was 15.4% in the 2000s, ranked 189th in the world, and was on a par with Pakistan (15.4%), Myanmar (15.3%).

The Solomon Islands gross fixed capital formation per capita was $145.9 in the 2000s, ranked 174th in the world. The gross fixed capital formation per capita in the Solomon Islands was less than gross fixed capital formation per capita in the world ($1 690.7) in 11.6 times, and was less than fixed capital formation per capita in Oceania ($6 596.9) in 45.2 times.

The growth of gross fixed capital formation in the Solomon Islands was 5.7% in the 2000s, ranked 91st in the world, and was on a par with Cuba (5.7%). The growth of gross fixed capital formation in the Solomon Islands (5.7%) was greater than growth of gross fixed capital formation in the world (3.5%), was greater than growth of fixed capital formation in Oceania (5.0%).

Comparison with neighbors. The Solomon Islands fixed capital formation was greater than in Nauru ($12.0 million); but less than in

New Caledonia ($2.0 billion), in Papua New Guinea ($1.3 billion), and in Vanuatu ($116.1 million). The fixed capital formation per capita in the Solomon Islands was less than in New Caledonia ($8.4 thousand), in Nauru ($1 196.3), in Vanuatu ($561.2), and in Papua New Guinea ($195.8). The growth of gross fixed capital formation in the Solomon Islands was greater than in Nauru (0.43%); but less than in Papua New Guinea (11.6%), in New Caledonia (8.6%), and in Vanuatu (8.0%).

Comparison with leaders. The gross fixed capital formation of the Solomon Islands was less than in the USA ($2.8 trillion), in Japan ($1.2 trillion), in China ($1.0 trillion), in Germany ($557.7 billion), and in France ($463.9 billion). The Solomon Islands gross fixed capital formation per capita was less than in the United States ($9.4 thousand), in Japan ($9.0 thousand), in France ($7.4 thousand), in Germany ($6.9 thousand), and in China ($782.2). The growth of gross fixed capital formation in the Solomon Islands was greater than in France (1.6%), in the United States (0.43%), in Germany (-0.56%), and in Japan (-2.0%); but less than in China (13.4%).

The 2010s

The Solomon Islands gross fixed capital formation was $162.3 million per year in the 2010s, ranked 193rd in the world, and was on a par with the Comoros ($161.9 million). The share in the world was 0.0008%, and 0.039% in Oceania.

The share of fixed capital formation in GDP of the Solomon Islands was 15.1% in the 2010s, ranked 190th in the world, and was on a par with the Comoros (15.3%).

The gross fixed capital formation per capita in the Solomon Islands was $272.1 in the 2010s, ranked 176th in the world. The Solomon Islands fixed capital formation per capita was less than gross fixed capital formation per capita in the world ($2 621.1) in 9.6 times, and was less than gross fixed capital formation per capita in Oceania ($10 543.6) in 38.7 times.

The growth of fixed capital formation in the Solomon Islands was -0.3% in the 2010s, ranked 176th in the world. The growth of gross fixed capital formation in the Solomon Islands (-0.29%) was less than growth of fixed capital formation in the world (4.1%), was less than growth of gross fixed capital formation in Oceania (1.3%).

Comparison with neighbors. The gross fixed capital formation of the Solomon Islands was 3.3 times higher than in Nauru ($49.2 million); but 22.7 times lower than in New Caledonia ($3.7 billion), 19.3 times lower than in Papua New Guinea ($3.1 billion), and 26.3% lower than in Vanuatu ($220.2 million). The gross fixed capital formation per capita in the Solomon Islands was 50.3 times lower than in New Caledonia ($13.7 thousand), 17.4 times lower than in Nauru ($4.7 thousand), 3.0 times lower than in Vanuatu ($822.6), and 30.2% lower than in Papua New Guinea ($390.1). The growth of fixed capital formation in the Solomon Islands was greater than in Papua New Guinea (-3.4%); but less than in Nauru (10.8%), in Vanuatu (0.72%), and in New Caledonia (-0.15%).

Comparison with leaders. The Solomon Islands fixed capital formation was 27 859.6 times lower than in China ($4.5 trillion), 22 169.7 times lower than in the United States ($3.6 trillion), 7 454.9 times lower than in Japan ($1.2 trillion), 4 635.4 times lower than in Germany ($752.5 billion), and 4 292.0 times lower than in India ($696.8 billion). The gross fixed capital formation per capita in the Solomon Islands was 41.4 times lower than in the USA ($11.3 thousand), 34.8 times lower than in Japan ($9.5 thousand), 33.8 times lower than in Germany ($9.2 thousand), 11.8 times lower than in China ($3.2 thousand), and 49.1% lower than in India ($535.2). The growth of gross fixed capital formation in the Solomon Islands was less than in China (8.0%), in India (5.8%), in the USA (3.8%), in Germany (2.8%), and in Japan (1.8%).